Charles H. Goren   e
Authority, holds   -
son in the annals of card play.

**This book—the most condensed
of Mr. Goren's many best sellers
on various aspects of bridge—
presents in simplified form the
methods currently employed by
90 percent of the most successful
bridge players today.**

THE FUNDAMENTALS
OF CONTRACT BRIDGE

is the work of a man who rates highest in international standing as a bridge teacher. His numerous books, his many lectures, his widely syndicated newspaper column and, of course, his record as a player are here distilled into a simple instruction manual guaranteed to improve the skills of any average bridge player.

THE FUNDAMENTALS
OF
CONTRACT BRIDGE

by CHARLES H. GOREN

POCKET BOOKS

New York   London   Toronto   Sydney   Tokyo

POCKET BOOKS, a division of Simon & Schuster Inc.
1230 Avenue of the Americas, New York, NY 10020

ISBN: 0-671-70460-5

First Pocket Books printing March 1955

57   56   55   54   53   52   51   50   49   48

POCKET and colophon are registered trademarks of
Simon & Schuster Inc.

Printed in the U.S.A.

foreword

This book concerns itself with just what its name implies, the fundamentals of contract bridge. It does not purport to be a guide for the absolute beginner, but rather presumes that the reader is already acquainted with the rudiments of the game. However, no attempt has been made to delve into the refinements and exceptions, with which only the advanced student should be concerned. I have contented myself with presenting in simplified form the methods currently employed by more than ninety per cent of the successful players of today. In bridge, as in other fields, time marches on. Many of the theories of a generation ago are no longer tenable. A decade of experience has made it clear that the bridge player must lay aside the tools with which he operated in pioneer days, just as fliers of today would spurn the planes that were considered air-worthy in the early thirties.

You will find here frequent references to point count in the matter of hand valuation. To some it may appear that a new system is being presented to them. But that is not the case. The methods outlined in this book are those that I have advocated for some time and represent, in codified form, the practices of the leading experts of today. I have reduced their practices, for purposes of instruction, to a simplified formula. This is the way they play, and I am sure that you can too.

In presenting this method I am confident, because in my travels to all corners of the nation in the past two years I have observed that it has taken hold as the easiest way to acquire proficiency in the game. The people have spoken, and it can no longer be disputed that this is the method of today.

contents

The Fundamentals
of Contract Bridge

opening suit bids of 1

Before approaching the subject of the opening bid, the student must acquaint himself with the table of values. First let us examine the point-count table:

THE POINT-COUNT TABLE

Ace	4
King	3
Queen	2
Jack	1

When valuing a hand for purposes of No Trump, we consider only high cards. But where a hand is being valued for the purpose of bidding a suit, distributional values must be taken into account. For purposes of computing the value of your hand at a suit bid, count your high cards, then add

  3 points if your hand contains a void,
  2 points if it contains a singleton,
  1 point for each doubleton.

You will hear frequent reference to defensive tricks, sometimes called "quick tricks." The following is the accepted table:

TABLE OF QUICK (DEFENSIVE) TRICKS

2 Quick Tricks	*1½ Quick Tricks*
A K	A Q

1 Quick Trick	*½ Quick Trick*
A	K x
K Q	
K J 10	

biddable suits

In order to open the bidding with one of a suit, a player should have what is known as a biddable suit. A biddable suit must contain at least four cards which must be headed by some high-card strength. A four-card suit that is headed by the Queen or better may be regarded as biddable, and any five-card suit, even without high-card strength, is considered biddable. A rebiddable suit is a good five-card suit. It is called rebiddable because a player holding it may repeat that suit on the next round without partner's having supported it. A good five-card suit is considered to be one that has at least two of the important honors. For example:

K Q 10 x x

requirements for the opening suit bid of 1

Those who employ honor tricks express the requirement as follows:

Two and one half honor tricks with a rebiddable suit or three honor tricks with a non-rebiddable suit.

However, it is easier to express the requirement for an opening bid in terms of point count, and here is what they are:

If your hand contains 12 points (including high cards and distribution), you *may* open if you have a very good five-card suit.

If your hand contains 13 points, it is considered an optional opening. You may open it if you find it convenient to do so; that is, if your next bid will not prove embarrassing to you.

If your hand contains 14 points, you *must* open.

the new-suit forcing principle

The opening bidder should be aware of the most important convention in contract bridge, which is this: When opener bids 1 of a suit and responder names any new suit, opener must bid again if responder has not previously passed.

third- and fourth-hand bidding

In the early days of contract the requirements for third- and fourth-hand openings were higher than those for first and second hand. Present-day practices are different. If a hand is worth a bid, it should be bid in any position at the table. As a matter of fact, in third position hands may be opened with a little less strength. Where the third hand has a good suit, he may open with as little as 11 points, but then he need not bid again when his partner names a new suit.

In fourth hand, any sound opening bid should be opened.

which suit to bid first?

If you have two five-card suits, you should bid first the one which is higher-ranking, even though the other may be a stronger suit. For example, you hold:

♠ Q 10 x x x   ♡ A K x x x   ◇ x   ♣ x x

You open the bidding with 1 Spade. If partner responds with 2 Clubs or 2 Diamonds, you will then rebid 2 Hearts. If partner wishes to return to your first suit, he may do so by bidding 2 Spades without increasing the contract.

With suits of unequal length, bid first the longer one.

If you have two biddable suits, one of five cards and the other of four, bid the five-card suit first. Here, length takes precedence over strength.[1] Example:

♠ A K Q J   ♡ A J x x x   ◇ K x x   ♣ x

Bid 1 Heart. When you mention Spades on the next round, partner will recognize that you have more Hearts than you have Spades.

[1]There is an exception to this rule with which I do not wish to burden the memory of the student at this point.

Similarly, if you have two biddable suits, one of six cards and one of five cards, bid the six-card suit first and then the five-card suit twice.
You hold:

♠ x   ♡ A K x x x   ◇ A Q x x x x   ♣ x

With this hand your correct opening is 1 Diamond. Responder bids 1 Spade. You bid 2 Hearts. At this point, partner is under the impression that you have five Diamonds and four Hearts. But that impression will soon be corrected. Over your 2 Heart bid, let us suppose responder bids 2 No Trump. Now, you must not bid 3 Diamonds; you must bid 3 Hearts. This is the only way to show your partner that you have five Hearts, because four-card suits are not rebid unless supported by partner. When your partner finds that you have five Hearts, he will know that you have six Diamonds, because you bid them first.

OPENING WITH FOUR-CARD SUITS

If you have no five-card suit, look for the shortest suit in your hand (singleton or doubleton) and bid first that suit ranking next below your singleton or doubleton. If the suit which ranks next below is not biddable, bid the next suit below that. For the purpose of this rule you should consider that Spades rank next below Clubs. In other words, where your singleton is Clubs, open with 1 Spade. For example, you hold:

♠ x x   ♡ A Q J x   ◇ A K J x   ♣ x x x

Bid 1 Heart, the suit below the doubleton. If partner bids 2 Clubs, your rebid is 2 Diamonds.
You hold:

♠ x x   ♡ x x x   ◇ A Q J x   ♣ A K J x

Bid 1 Diamond. The doubleton is Spades; the suit below is Hearts. But since your Heart suit is not biddable, you bid the next below that.

You hold:

♠ A Q J x ♡ x x ◊ A K J x ♣ J x x

Bid 1 Diamond, the suit below the doubleton.

You hold:

♠ A Q J x ♡ J x x ◊ A K J x ♣ x x

Bid 1 Spade. The doubleton is Clubs. The suit below Clubs for the purpose of this rule is Spades.

THE SHORT-CLUB BID

This is not a convention, but a convenient device for taking care of awkward hands. Where the normal bid might prove embarrassing, you may find it more convenient to open with 1 Club, permitting partner to respond at a low level. At this point I offer you this heartfelt advice. Never be heard to inquire: "Partner, do you play the short Club?" It is the surest way to have yourself stamped as a member of the uninitiated. And if anyone naïvely asks you whether you play the short Club, reply firmly in the negative. Otherwise he will accuse you of not having Clubs any time you bid the suit. What you might say, but for the fact that it would violate the social amenities, is, "Partner, you take care of your business and I'll look after mine."

♠ J 10 x x ♡ Q x x x ◊ A x ♣ A K x (14)

This hand containing 14 points is a mandatory opening, and the only convenient way to get the bidding started is with 1 Club. Note that both your 4-card major suits are not robust and you do not particularly desire to bid either of them unless partner can bid them. If partner bids either suit, you have a natural raise.

You hold:

♠ A K J x   ♡ x x x   ◇ x x x   ♣ A Q x   (14)

Here again you have 14 points and must open, but it will be inconvenient to bid 1 Spade. What will you rebid if partner responds with 2 Diamonds? Therefore, open 1 Club and rebid 1 Spade if partner responds with a red suit.

opening no trump bids

Ace	4
King	3
Queen	2
Jack	1

The pack contains 40 points (10 points in each suit). A partnership will normally be able to make game (3 No Trump) with a combined holding of 26 points. However, if one of the partners holds a long suit, the game may be won with a little less than 26 points.

To qualify as an opening No Trump bid, a hand must have not only the right size, but the right shape. Such openings should be made only with hands of the No Trump family. There are three members of that family. And these are the shapes:

4-3-3-3
4-4-3-2
5-3-3-2

A No Trump opening should not be made with a hand containing a worthless doubleton. The doubleton should be headed by one of the high honors.

So much for the shape. Now for the size:

An opening Bid of 1 No Trump Shows a Count of 16 to 18.

The student will observe that if a hand counts 20 or 21, it is too big for 1 No Trump. This does not mean that it should be opened with a bid of 2 No Trump, for in a moment we shall see that an opening 2 No Trump bid requires 22 points. But these 20- and 21-point hands should be opened with a bid of 1 of a suit. Opener will show his true colors on the next round by jumping the bid in No Trump.

Examples of opening bids of 1 No Trump:

♠ K J x   ♡ A x x   ◇ K Q J x   ♣ Q J x   (17)

♠ Q x x x   ♡ 10 x x   ◇ A K Q   ♣ A Q x   (17)

A 1 No Trump opening (17 points) with three suits stopped:

♠ J x x x   ♡ A x x x   ◇ K x   ♣ A K x   (15)

This hand has all suits stopped but is short of the high-card requirement for an opening bid of 1 No Trump. It has only 15 points. It is better, therefore, to get the bidding started with an introductory bid of 1 Club.

♠ K Q x   ♡ A x x   ◇ K x x   ♣ A K J x   (20)

This hand contains 20 points and is above the limit of a 1 No Trump bid. It should therefore be opened with 1 Club, with the bidder intending to jump in No Trump over partner's response.

opening bid of 2 no trump

This bid describes a hand of the No Trump family —with all four suits protected and a point count of 22, 23, or 24:

♠ A J x   ♡ A K x   ◇ A K x x   ♣ K J x   (23)

♠ K J x   ♡ A Q   ◇ A Q J x x   ♣ K Q x   (22)

opening bid of 3 no trump

This bid describes a hand of the No Trump family —with all four suits protected and a point count of 25, 26, or 27:

♠ A Q J   ♡ A Q 10   ◇ K Q x   ♣ A K x x   (25)

responses to no trump bids

WITH BALANCED HANDS

Responses to opening bids of 1 No Trump: Remember that it normally takes 26 points to produce 3 No Trump—with a five-card suit 25 will suffice.

Raise 1 No Trump to 2 No Trump with 8 or 9 points (you may raise with a point less if you have a fairly good five-card suit). With less than this, pass.

Raise 1 No Trump to 3 No Trump with 10 to 14 points.

A partnership holding of 33 points will usually produce a small slam.

A partnership holding of 37 points will usually produce a grand slam.

In all the following examples your partner opens with 1 No Trump. You hold:

♠ K x x x x ♡ Q x x ◇ J x ♣ x x x (6)

Pass. You have only 6 points and a balanced hand.

♠ J x   ♡ K Q x x x   ◇ K x x   ♣ x x x   (9)

Raise to 2 No Trump. You have a balanced hand with 9 points.

♠ K x x x   ♡ A x x   ◇ x x x   ♣ x x x   (7)

Pass. You have only 7 points.

♠ K x x   ♡ x x   ◇ x x x   ♣ A 10 x x x   (7)

Raise to 2 No Trump. A raise may be given with 7 points if you have a fairly good five-card suit.

♠ A x x   ♡ Q x   ◇ Q J x x   ♣ K J x x   (13)

Raise to 3 No Trump. You have a count of 13. There is no reasonable hope for a slam, since the partnership's maximum is 32.

♠ A x x   ♡ K x x   ◇ Q x x   ♣ J x x x   (10)

Raise to 3 No Trump. You have a count of 10. The partnership is assured of at least 26 points.

♠ A 10 x   ♡ Q J x   ◇ A K x   ♣ J 10 x x   (15)

Raise to 4 No Trump. The count is 15. If partner has a minimum, he should pass. If he has a near maximum, you will have a slam.

♠ K J x   ♡ A x x x   ◇ K Q x   ♣ A 10 x   (17)

Raise to 6 No Trump. You have a good No Trump bid, facing a No Trump opening. Your 17, plus partner's announced minimum of 16, brings the total to at least 33. But since it cannot be more than 36, you abandon the try for a grand slam.

suit responses to opening bid of 1 no trump

TAKE-OUT TO 2 OF A MINOR SUIT

A response of 2 in a minor suit denotes the inability to give a raise in No Trump and therefore indicates a hand with less than 7 points. Holding the high-card content for a raise to 2 No Trump, responder must never bid 2 Clubs or 2 Diamonds, but should raise the No Trump even with a singleton or a six-card suit.

The take-out to 2 of a minor is made on two types of hands:

1. Hopeless hands which have no future but must be played in the minor suit.

2. Hands which are just short of the requirements for a raise but are a little too good to pass; that is, hands containing a five-card suit with 6 points. For example, partner opens with 1 No Trump. You hold:

♠ none ♡ x x x ◇ x x x x ♣ Q J x x x

Bid 2 Clubs, intending to bid 3 Clubs as the "final" bid if partner rebids 2 No Trump.

♠ K x ♡ x x x ◇ x x x ♣ K 10 x x x (6)

Respond 2 Clubs. If partner has an absolute maximum No Trump, there may be a chance for game.

TAKE-OUT TO 2 OF A MAJOR SUIT

This take-out is treated somewhat differently from a take-out to 2 of a minor. A take-out of 2 in a major is in a sense ambiguous. It may be made on a hand which possesses the count for a raise to 2 No Trump but on which responder thinks might play better in a suit. He therefore responds with 2 in a major. Opener is not expected to pass unless he has only 16 points. If opener raises the major, responder will go to 4. If opener rebids 2 No Trump, responder expects to take him to game.

Partner opens with 1 No Trump. You hold:

♠ x   ♥ A Q J x x   ♦ x x x   ♣ J x x x

Bid 2 Hearts. You have the count for a raise to 2 No Trump (8 points), but your hand is unbalanced and may play better in Hearts. This will give partner the choice.

Where your hand is a member of the No Trump family—that is, it does not contain a void, a singleton, or 2 doubletons—it is usually superior to raise the No Trump, if you have the proper count, even though your suit happens to be a major. For instance:

Partner opens with 1 No Trump. You hold:

♠ x x   ♥ K Q x x x   ♦ K x x   ♣ x x x   (8)

With this evenly balanced hand, while the response of 2 Hearts may be employed, it is better tactics to raise the No Trump (point count 8) and try for the nine-trick game.

A take-out of 2 of a suit, major or minor, may be made with a weak hand containing a long suit where you feel that the hand must play in that suit. But in this case you must repeat your suit at the level of 3. If you take out to 2 of a suit and partner rebids 2 No Trump, and then you bid 3 of the same suit, your partner is under compulsion to quit. For example, you hold:

♠ Q 10 x x x x x   ♥ x   ♦ x x   ♣ J x x

Respond 2 Spades. If partner bids 2 No Trump, rebid 3 Spades. Opener must resign.

TAKE-OUT TO 4 OF A MAJOR

A leap to 4 Hearts or 4 Spades over a 1 No Trump opening indicates a hand with a long suit, at least six cards, and less than 10 points in high cards. Responder should be able to develop slightly more than five tricks in his own hand with that suit as trump. For example, partner opens with 1 No Trump. You hold:

♠ K 10 9 x x x ♡ x x ◇ K x x x ♣ x

Bid 4 Spades. Opposite a No Trump opening, your hand will develop more than five tricks between the long Spades and the Diamond suit. Opener is required to pass, since your leap to 4 in a major denies the high-card values necessary for a slam.

TAKE-OUT TO 3 OF A SUIT

This type of bid is made on a hand that possesses the high-card values for a raise to 3 No Trump (that is, at least 10 points), and responder either feels that the hand might play better in the suit or is using this bid as a preliminary step to try for a slam.

Partner opens with 1 No Trump. You hold:

1. ♠ A Q 10 x x ♡ K Q x ◇ x x x x ♣ x (11)
2. ♠ x ♡ A Q J x x ◇ x x ♣ A Q J 10 x (14)

On No. 1, respond 3 Spades. You have the ingredients of a raise to 3 No Trump (11 points in high cards), but your hand is unbalanced and you prefer to play a suit. With No. 2, bid 3 Hearts. Your hand is unbalanced and, moreover, you will make an effort to reach a slam by trying 4 Clubs next round if partner rebids 3 No Trump.

responses to opening bids of 2 no trump

WITH BALANCED HANDS

Always add your points to those shown by partner's opening (in this instance, 22).

With 4 to 8 points, raise to 3 No Trump. You know there is no slam since the most partner can have is 24 points (24 plus 8 equals 32).

With 9 points, raise to 4 No Trump. There may be a slam if partner has the maximum of 24 points (24 plus 9 equals 33).

With 10 points, there will be a slam unless partner has a minimum (22 points). Therefore, first bid a suit and then raise to 4 No Trump. Bidding a suit and then raising to 4 No Trump is stronger than just bidding 4 No Trump.

With 11 or 12 points, bid 6 No Trump.

With 13 or 14 points, first bid a suit and then bid 6 No Trump. This is stronger than just bidding 6 No Trump directly. It asks partner to bid 7 if he has a maximum.

With 15 points, you may bid 7 No Trump (22 plus 15 equals 37).

responses to opening bids of 2 no trump

WITH UNBALANCED HANDS

1. Bid any six-card major suit regardless of the high-card content of your hand.

2. Bid any five-card major suit if your hand contains at least 4 points in high cards.

3. Jump to 4 in a major suit with a six-card suit and a hand containing about 8 points in high cards.

4. Do not show minor suits unless the hand has slam possibilities. Even with six-card minor suits, the No Trump should be raised instead.

responses to opening bids of 3 no trump

The same principles are applicable here as in the responses to 2 No Trump openings. Only, in this case, partner is known to have 25 to 27 points. Add your points to his, keeping your eye on the figure 33 for a small slam and 37 for a grand slam. This bidding assumes a balanced hand. With a very long suit you may make the grade with somewhat less in point count.

There is no such thing as a "rescue" bid when partner opens with 3 No Trump. Therefore, any response is construed as a slam try. With a five-card biddable suit and a point count of 5, bid that suit. Any reasonably good six-card suit should be shown at the 4 level. With a balanced hand and a point count of 7, raise to 4 No Trump, which partner will pass if he has only 25.

Partner opens with 3 No Trump. You hold:

♠ K Q x x x ♡ x x ◇ x x x ♣ x x x

Bid 4 Spades (a five-card biddable suit with a high-card count of 5).

♠ x x x ♡ J x x ◇ K x x ♣ K x x

Raise to 4 No Trump (point count of 7).

♠ Q J x   ♡ A x x   ♢ Q 10 x   ♣ A 10 x x

Bid 7 No Trump (13 points). You are assured of a combined holding of 38 points.

rebids by opening no trumper

If you have opened with 1 No Trump, you should pass in several instances:

1. When partner raises to 3 No Trump.

2. When partner jumps to 4 Hearts or 4 Spades.

3. When partner raises to 2 No Trump, if you have only 16 points.

4. When partner takes out to 2 Hearts or 2 Spades, if you have only 16 points.

5. When partner takes out to 2 Clubs or 2 Diamonds, unless you have a maximum No Trump, or are able to raise partner's suit to 3 with two high honors in his suit.

rebids when partner responds 2 clubs or 2 diamonds

Unless opener holds a maximum, he should pass, for partner is known to have less than 7 points. However, where the No Trump opener has two high honors in the responder's suit, he should raise to 3 of the minor. This may permit responder to go on to 3 No Trump with a very weak hand since he knows that a six-card suit can be run against the opposition. For example:

NORTH	SOUTH
♠ K J x	♠ x x
♡ Q J x	♡ x x
◇ A x x x	◇ K x x
♣ A K x	♣ Q 10 x x x x

Over North's 1 No Trump bid, South bids 2 Clubs, denying the high-card requirement of a raise to 2 No Trump. North, having a near maximum (18 points), indicates that, as well as two honors in Clubs, by raising to 3 Clubs. Responder, with the knowledge that he can run six Club tricks, returns to 3 No Trump, for which there must be a good play.

opening 2 bids (in a suit)

An opening bid of 2 in a suit is an absolute demand for game. It forces both the opener and his partner, who are considered to have entered into an agreement to play at a final game contract, unless the opposition chooses to deprive them of the privilege. In that case the enemy must be made to pay for the affront by a penalty double. Since responder may have nothing, opener should have game in his own hand (all but one trick). For instance, the hand must contain at least 9 winners in a major suit and 10 winners with a minor suit as trump. The high-card requirement for such a bid is at least four honor tricks, provided you have within a trick of game in your own hand. Remember, it takes about 26 points to produce game. If you open with a 2 demand bid, you should have at least 25 of them in your own hand, unless you have a very long suit. On a point-count basis, which must include the requirements outlined above, the following table will serve as a well-nigh foolproof guide:

1. With a good five-card suit—25 points.
2. With a good six-card suit—23 points.

3. With a good seven-card suit—21 points.

4. With a second good five-card suit—1 point less than above.

You hold:

♠ A K x x   ♡ A K x x   ◇ x   ♣ A K x x

This hand is worth 23 points, 21 in high cards and 2 for distribution. Bid 1 Club. Don't consider a demand bid despite your six honor tricks. If partner has nothing, you will have no game.

♠ A K Q J x x x   ♡ A x x   ◇ A x   ♣ x

This hand contains 21 points and a good seven-card suit and fulfills the other requirements; namely, nine winners in a major suit and four or more honor tricks.

responses to opening 2 bids (in a suit)

Some players labor under the erroneous belief that when responder holds a bust hand and responds with 2 No Trump he has then discharged his obligations. That is not the case. He must keep responding until the hand is ultimately played at a game contract, unless the opponents in the meantime have been doubled. The conventional response with a weak hand is 2 No Trump. This response does not describe the type of hand but announces its lack of point count; for example:

♠ x x   ♡ x x   ◇ Q J 10 x x x x   ♣ x x

In response to an opening bid of 2 Hearts, bid 2 No Trump, intending to bid Diamonds later, so that partner will realize that, while you have length in Diamonds, you have little high-card value.

The natural response may take the following forms:

1. A raise in partner's suit.	The minimum requirement in each case is 7 points if the hand contains 1 quick trick, or 8 points if the hand contains only one half a quick trick.
2. An ordinary suit take-out.	
3. A response of 3 No Trump.	

Bear in mind that the responder may have trump support, or a good suit of his own, or Aces and Kings. All three are of prime importance, and perhaps the most important is the trump support.

Partner opens with 2 Hearts. You hold:

♠ x x   ♡ J 10 x x   ◇ K Q J   ♣ x x x x

Bid 3 Hearts. Your hand is worth about 9 points in support of Hearts. The single raise may also be given with stronger hands, when responder expects to do considerable bidding on subsequent rounds. The purpose is immediately to establish the trump and encourage descriptive bidding. Such descriptive bidding will be outlined in the chapter on slams.

Where responder has 7 points and a biddable suit, the suit should be shown as a natural response. I advise against responding with very weak suits and suggest that a five-card suit be headed by at least Q-J. Lacking both trump support and a biddable suit, but a hand containing at least 8 points, respond with 3 No Trump. Such hands will usually produce a slam, for the opener presumably has 25 points, which, added to your 8, amounts to 33.

Partner opens with 2 Hearts. You hold:

♠ K J 10xx   ♡ Kx   ◇ xxx   ♣ xxx

Respond 2 Spades, a natural bid, showing a Spade suit and a little over 7 points.

♠ K Q x   ♡ J 10x   ◇ J 10xxx   ♣ xx

Respond 3 Hearts, a natural bid, showing normal trump support and 8 points in support of partner's 2 Heart bid. The Diamond suit is too weak to bother with.

♠ A Kxx   ♡ xxx   ◇ xx   ♣ K J xx

Respond 2 Spades, a natural bid, showing a Spade suit. On this particular hand you will surely reach a slam and you are merely awaiting developments. You have 11 points in high cards alone, and partner's hand is presumably worth at least 25 points, so that the total is at least 36.

pre-emptive bids

An opening pre-emptive bid is a call of 3, 4, or 5 of a suit and denotes a hand that is weak in high-card count. A pre-emptive bidder expects to suffer a loss which he is willing to incur in order to confuse the opposition. Opening pre-emptive bids are made with the sole purpose of disrupting the opponents' communications. Do not pre-empt on any hand that contains as many as 11 points in high cards (exclusive of distribution). Don't open with a 3 bid if you have a good hand just because you have a long suit. With a good hand you would like to get your partner interested in a conversation, and it is very difficult for him to speak at such a high level.

When you make a pre-emptive bid, you risk the loss of 500 points—that is, you expect to be down 2 if vulnerable, 3 if not vulnerable.

You hold:

♠ K Q J 10 x x x x   ♡ x x   ◇ x x   ♣ x

If not vulnerable, bid 4 Spades, an overbid of three tricks. If vulnerable, bid 3 Spades, an overbid of two tricks.

quiz no. 1: opening bids

(Answers follow this quiz)

1. ♠ x x x ♡ A K x x ◇ A x x ♣ x x x

   What is your opening bid?

2. ♠ A J x x ♡ A K Q x ◇ x x x ♣ x x

   What is your opening bid?

3. ♠ J 10 x x ♡ A Q x ◇ A Q x ♣ A K x

   What is your opening bid?

4. ♠ J x x ♡ K Q 10 x ◇ A Q x ♣ A J x

   What is your opening bid?

5. ♠ A x x ♡ K x ◇ A K J x x ♣ Q x x

   What is your opening bid?

6. ♠ Q 10 x x   ♡ K 10 x x   ◇ x   ♣ A Q x x

   What is your opening bid?

7. ♠ A Q x x x   ♡ A K x   ◇ A K x   ♣ x x

   What is your opening bid?

8. ♠ J 10 x x   ♡ A K x x x   ◇ Q x x   ♣ A

   What is your opening bid?

9. ♠ K Q J x   ♡ A Q 10 x x   ◇ x x   ♣ x x

   What is your opening bid?

10. ♠ Q x x x x   ♡ A K J x x   ◇ x   ♣ K x

    What is your opening bid?

11. As dealer you hold:

    ♠ A K Q J x x x   ♡ A x   ◇ x   ♣ A x x

    What do you bid?

12. As dealer you hold:

    ♠ A K J x x   ♡ A   ◇ A K x   ♣ K Q 10 x

    What do you bid?

13. As dealer you hold:

    ♠ A Q x x x   ♡ A K x   ◇ A Q x   ♣ K x

    What do you bid?

14. As dealer you hold:

♠ A K x x   ♡ A K x x   ◇ x   ♣ A K x x

What do you bid?

15. As dealer you hold:

♠ A K J 9 x x   ♡ A Q 10 x x   ◇ A K
   ♣ none

What do you bid?

16. As dealer you hold:

♠ A K J 10 9   ♡ A K Q x x   ◇ x   ♣ K x

What do you bid?

17. As dealer you hold:

♠ A x   ♡ A x   ◇ K Q   ♣ A K Q x x x x

What do you bid?

18. As dealer you hold:

♠ A K J   ♡ A K Q 10   ◇ A K   ♣ A Q J x

What do you bid?

19. You are dealer, not vulnerable, and hold:

♠ K Q J x x x   ♡ x   ◇ x x x   ♣ x x

What is your opening bid?

20. As dealer you hold:

♠ A K J 10 x x x x   ♡ x   ◇ x x   ♣ x x

What is your opening bid?

21. As dealer you hold:

    ♠ A K Q J x x x ♡ x ◇ A x x ♣ x x

What is your opening bid?

22. As dealer you hold:

    ♠ A K Q x x x ♡ Q x x ◇ x x ♣ x x

What is your opening bid?

answers to quiz no. 1

1. Pass. This hand contains only 11 points. No rebid is available if partner responds with 2 Clubs or 2 Diamonds.

2. 1 Spade, the suit below the doubleton. A Heart bid is improper. It affords no convenient rebid if partner responds with 2 of a minor suit.

3. 1 Club. This hand is the proper type for a 1 No Trump bid, but it is too strong, containing 20 points, yet is not quite big enough for an opening 2 No Trump bid. Therefore, bid 1 Club, intending to jump into No Trump on the next round.

4. 1 No Trump. The point count is 17, with three suits stopped. This hand contains exactly four honor tricks, counting the plus values, and the 4–3–3 distribution is of the No Trump variety.

5. 1 No Trump. The 5–3–3–2 distribution is in the No Trump family, all suits are stopped, and you have 17 points, which meets the requirement. If you bid 1

Diamond, you will be in a quandary if partner responds with 1 Heart, for your hand will be a bit too weak for a rebid of 2 No Trump, but too strong for a rebid of 2 Diamonds or 1 No Trump. Take only half credit if your answer was 1 Diamond.

6. 1 Club. This hand contains a high-card point count of only 11, but the distributional features—that is, the singleton—account for an additional 2 points, bringing it to a total of 13. This makes it an optional opening bid. The option should be exercised because of the possession of eight cards in the major suits and the ease with which a rebid can be made.

7. 1 Spade. Take no credit at all if your answer was 2 Spades because of the five and one half quick tricks. Such a bid would be forcing to game and, if partner had nothing, might lead to disaster. You cannot promise nine winners.

8. 1 Heart, and you do not bid Spades but only support Spades if partner bids the suit.

9. 1 Spade. On opening bids of moderate strength where you have touching suits in which the lower-ranking suit is longer than the higher-ranking, you pretend that you do not possess the fifth card in the longer suit and treat both as if they were each four-card suits. This is done for the convenience it affords in rebidding. You open with 1 Spade and you then have a natural rebid in your Heart suit. This permits partner to take a preference at one level lower if he prefers your first-bid suit.

10. 1 Spade. With touching biddable suits of equal length, you always bid the higher-ranking because it

permits an easy natural rebid. If you chose to bid the Heart suit because it was stronger, take a demerit.

11. This is an ideal hand which meets the requirements for an opening 2 demand bid which is forcing to game on both members of the partnership. With a seven-card suit you need 21 points, and this hand has 18 in high cards, 2 points for the singleton, and 1 for the doubleton. In addition, it has the value of the long cards in the trump suit named. It further meets the requirements of four top honor tricks and has exactly four losers, which is just one trick short of game.

12. 2 Spades. This hand has 24 points in high cards and 2 for distribution by virtue of the singleton. With a good five-card suit the requirement for opening with a 2 bid is 25 points.

13. Since you cannot guarantee nine winners with this mediocre Spade suit, you cannot open with a 2 demand bid despite the wealth of high cards. If partner should happen to be "busted," you might find the taking of nine tricks a difficult proposition. This hand meets the exact requirement for a 2 No Trump opening bid, and that should be your call.

14. Despite the possession of six honor tricks, this hand does not warrant opening with a 2 demand bid. You cannot guarantee nine winners with this holding. This hand is valued at only 23 points.

15. 2 Spades. This hand undoubtedly meets the requirements. You will bid Hearts on the next round, and if partner sounds at all encouraging in either one of your suits you should bid a slam in that denomination.

16. 2 Spades. If partner should have just three small cards in either one of your major suits, making game should not be a difficult proposition. On this holding a reasonable estimate of the losers is 1 Diamond, 1 Club, and 1 in either of your major suits, which brings you to a total of ten winners. With two good suits, a 2 bid may be made with a point or two less than the normal requirement.

17. This is an ideal hand for opening with a 2 demand bid in a minor suit. You have ten winners, and if partner shows no enthusiasm and persists in signing off by answering No Trump, your hand will be an ideal dummy for a 3 No Trump contract, where your hand alone should take 9 or 10 tricks.

18. Here you have a hand that is much too strong to open with 3 No Trump. The top limit for that call is 27 points, and you hold 30. This is the only case in which you are permitted to open with a 2 demand bid when the longest suit in your hand is four cards. Bid 2 Hearts.

19. 3 Spades. That call shows a hand able to take six tricks as declarer, principally in the suit named and with very little in the way of defense.

20. Bid 4 Spades. An opening bid of 4 in a major denotes the ability to take eight tricks, with practically all of them in the suit named and little, if any, outside strength.

21. Bid 1 Spade. Do not pre-empt. Although you have eight tricks in hand, the possession of a side ace, which adds to your defensive strength and promotes the possibilities of a slam, would bar this holding as a pre-emptive bid.

22. Bid 1 Spade. Do not pre-empt. This hand is too good for a pre-emptive bid of 3. It might be a suitable dummy for a 3 No Trump contract, for instance, or for a Heart contract, if partner should happen to have a long suit there.

responses

responding with weak hands

When partner opens with 1 of a suit, you should make an effort to keep the bidding alive, even with a relatively weak hand, if you are in a position to do so without increasing the level of the contract. This may be done by responding with:

1. 1 NO TRUMP ON A BALANCED HAND, CONTAINING 6 TO 9 POINTS.

2. 1 OF A SUIT. This may be done with as little as 6 points, including points allowed for distribution.

3. Where you have some support for partner's suit, you may keep the bidding open with a relatively weak hand by offering partner a single raise in his suit. This bid has a slightly wider range—it may be anywhere from 6 to 10 points. This includes points assigned both for high cards and for distribution (that is, doubletons, singletons, and voids). These are known as "dummy points." For the scale of "dummy points," see page 46.

the response of 1 no trump

Bear in mind that in making No Trump responses of any kind only high-card values are counted. Do not, for the purpose of this response, consider distribution. Therefore, no points are assigned for doubletons and singletons.

Where you have at least 6 points in high cards, it is your duty to keep the bidding alive. This should be done by a bid of 1 No Trump, if that happens to be the cheapest available bid. It may also be done on a hand containing as many as 9 points, but not more. With more than 9 points, some other response should be chosen.

Partner opens with 1 Spade:

♠ xxx   ♡ Kxxx   ◊ Qxx   ♣ xxx

Pass. You have only 5 points in high cards and should not respond with 1 No Trump.

♠ xxx   ♡ Jxx   ◊ Axxx   ♣ Axx

Respond 1 No Trump. You have 9 points. This is the maximum high-card holding on which the 1 No Trump response may be made. The addition of any other value would make it obligatory for you to make some other response. In other words, holding more than 9 points, you should make a decided effort to get partner to speak again. Remember, when you respond with 1 No Trump, partner may pass and frequently does.

♠ xx   ♡ xxx   ◊ Kxx   ♣ KJxxx

Respond 1 No Trump. You have 7 points. The hand is not strong enough to justify increasing the contract to 2 Clubs.

free bids of 1 no trump

When partner opens the bidding and next hand overcalls, you are no longer burdened with the responsibility of keeping the bidding alive. A bid of 1 No Trump in that circumstance, therefore, indicates strength. In addition to guaranteeing protection in the adverse bid suit, it shows a high-card value ranging from 10 to 12 points. A free bid of 1 No Trump shows a hand that is not quite so strong as a 2 No Trump response (13 to 15), but stronger than the maximum courtesy response of 1 No Trump (6 to 9 points). For example, partner opens with 1 Diamond; next hand bids 1 Heart. You hold:

♠ J x x   ♡ A x x   ◇ x x x   ♣ K x x x

Pass. You have a count of only 8, and a free bid of 1 No Trump is not in order. Had second hand passed, you would have kept the bidding open with 1 No Trump.

♠ K x x   ♡ A J x   ◇ x x x   ♣ K x x x

Bid 1 No Trump over the adverse Heart bid. You have a count of 11. Remember, a free bid of 1 No Trump denotes a good hand.

the 1-over-1 response

We have observed that a response of 1 No Trump may be made with as little as 6 points. Contrary to popular belief, a response of 1 in a suit may be made with just as little. In fact, a response of 1 in a suit may be made with less high-card strength, for some of the points may consist of distribution. This must not be confused with the response of 2 in a suit, for which greater values must be held.

With a weak hand, the cheapest response is the best response, and 1 of a suit is cheaper than 1 No Trump. Therefore, *do not respond with 1 No Trump when able to respond with 1 in a suit.*

♠ x x ♡ K x x ◇ K J x x x ♣ x x x

If partner opens with 1 Club, you should respond with 1 Diamond. That is a cheaper response than 1 No Trump. For purposes of bidding Diamonds, your hand is worth 8 points (7 in high cards and 1 for the doubleton).

But if partner opens with 1 Spade, your proper response is 1 No Trump, the cheapest bid available. Your hand is not strong enough to justify a 2 Diamond response, which would require at least 10 points.

♠ x x x ♡ K J x x x x ◇ x x ♣ x x

Partner opens with 1 Club. Respond 1 Heart even though you have only 4 points in high cards. For purposes of bidding Hearts, your hand is worth 2 additional points for distribution, 1 for each doubleton. It is therefore worth 6 points and justifies a response at the level of 1.

But if partner opens with 1 Spade, you should pass. You are obviously not strong enough to increase the level to 2 Hearts, and you have not the 6 high-card points required for a response of 1 No Trump.

♠ Q x x ♡ 10 x x x ◇ K J x x ♣ x x

Partner opens with 1 Club. Respond 1 Diamond, not 1 No Trump. With a point count of 6, it is

obligatory for you to make a response. With this weak
hand, 1 Diamond is the cheapest bid available. It has
the merit of permitting partner to bid again at the
level of 1. If you mistakenly respond with 1 No
Trump, partner can no longer bid again at the same
level, and it may be that you have prevented him
from showing a four-card Heart suit which he was
afraid to bid at the higher level.

free bids at the level of 1

In the foregoing discussion it was assumed that
partner opened and second hand passed. You are
permitted to keep the bidding open at the level of 1
with extremely light holdings, but when second hand
speaks, any bid by you, even at the level of 1, shows
a hand which contains at least 9 points; in other
words, a fairly good hand.

the single raise

The raise from 1 to 2 of partner's suit has a fairly
wide range. It may be made on a rather weak hand
containing 6 points, or a fairly good hand containing
10 points. In any event, it is used to describe a hand
that is "fair to middling," but not a strong hand. In
order to give a single raise, responder must have
normal trump support; that is: x-x-x-x, or Q-x-x, or
J-x-x. Unless it is otherwise proven, he must assume
that partner holds a four-card suit.

If partner rebids the suit, you are to assume that it
is a five-card suit, and normal trump support becomes
x-x-x, or Q-x. If partner bids a suit for the third time

without your having supported it, you may assume he holds six and you may raise with only two small trumps or the singleton Queen. Generally speaking, the partnership should hold at least eight trumps to make it a convenient vehicle.

"dummy points"

In raising partner's suit bid, one must compute the value of the hand (a) in high cards, (b) in short suits. High cards are computed at their face value.

Valuing short suits in responder's hand:

> *Add 1 point for each doubleton.*
> *Add 3 points for each singleton.*
> *Add 5 points for a void.*

(Note the difference in valuation of short suits between the opening bidder's hand and the responder's hand.) Certain deductions are made when holding a hand, which may be dummy, which contains a flaw:

1. Possession of only three trumps when raising partner's suit is a flaw.

2. A 4-3-3-3 distribution is a flaw when raising partner's suit.[1]

♠ A x x x   ♡ x x x x   ◇ x x   ♣ J x x

Partner opens with 1 Heart. Raise to 2. You have normal trump support and 6 points in support of a Heart bid, 5 in high cards and 1 for the doubleton.

[1]There is a refinement employed by experienced players with which I do not at this point wish to confuse the student. It has to do with the promoted value of trump honors. The Jack of partner's suit is promoted to a Queen, the Queen is promoted to a King, and the King is promoted to an Ace.

♠ x x ♡ A x x x ◊ Q x x x ♣ x x x

Raise to 2 Hearts. Your hand is worth 7 points in support of a Heart bid, 6 in high cards and 1 for the doubleton Spade.

responding with good hands

1. Jump raise in partner's suit (1 Spade to 3 Spades). This bid is forcing to game and requires 13 to 16 "dummy points." Here we have an opening bid facing an opening bid.

2. Jump take-out in No Trump (1 Spade to 2 No Trump). This bid is forcing to game (13 to 15). Here again we have an opening bid facing an opening bid.

3. Jump in a new suit (that is, 1 Heart to 2 Spades, or 1 Heart to 3 Diamonds). This bid is forcing to game and suggests a slam (19 or more points).

4. Take-out into 2 of a new suit (1 Heart to 2 Diamonds). This bid increases the contract and is therefore encouraging. It is forcing for one round (10 or more points).

5. Take-out into 1 of a suit (1 Club to 1 Heart). This bid is ambiguous. It may prove encouraging or discouraging, depending upon developments. It is forcing for one round and contains anywhere from 6 to 18 points.

jump raise from 1 to 3

13 TO 16 POINTS

This is a demand for game (unless partner has previously passed, in which case opener may use his own judgment). Responder must have at least four trumps headed by the Jack or better. Three good trumps will not do. The hand must contain 13 to 16 points, counting high-card points and distributional values as a dummy hand. (In other words, responder's hand must be the equivalent of an opening bid, facing his partner's opening bid.)

Partner opens with 1 Spade. You hold:

♠ K J x x   ♡ A J x x   ◇ x x   ♣ A x x

Bid 3 Spades. Your hand contains 13 points in high cards and 1 distributional point for the doubleton. You have the required trump support and your hand is the equivalent of an opening bid.

Partner opens with 1 Heart. You hold:

♠ x x   ♡ K J x x   ◇ A x x   ♣ A J x x

You have the required trump support. Bid 3 Hearts. You have 13 points in high cards and 1 for the doubleton. Therefore, your hand totals 14 points, which is the equal of a good opening bid.

An opening bid, facing an opening bid, will produce game.

Partner bids 1 Spade. You hold:

♠ A x x x   ♡ x   ◇ K x x x   ♣ K x x x

Bid 3 Spades. You have the required trump support and the equal of an opening bid opposite a Spade bid. Your hand contains 10 points in high cards, which, added to the 3 points for the singleton Heart, gives you a total valuation of 13 points, which renders your hand the equal of an opening bid and therefore meets with the requirements for a jump raise.

raising from 1 to 4 in a major suit

This bid shows a hand with more than ample trump support, a singleton or void, but not more than 9 points in high cards.

Partner opens with 1 Spade. You hold:

♠ Q J x x x   ♡ x   ◊ K J x x x   ♣ x x

Bid 4 Spades. This hand contains only 7 points in high cards, has the required singleton and more than ample trump support.

♠ A 10 x x x   ♡ x   ◊ Q x   ♣ A J 10 x x

This hand is too strong for a 4 Spade response. Bid either 3 Spades or a temporary bid of 2 Clubs.

jump take-out in no trump

1 SPADE TO 2 NO TRUMP

This response is forcing to game and shows a hand with all unnamed suits protected, at least two cards in partner's suit, and a point count of 13 to 15 (in other words, the equal of an opening bid). For example:

Partner opens with 1 Spade. You hold:

♠ x x x   ♡ Q 10 x   ◊ K J x x   ♣ A K x

Respond 2 No Trump (13 points, all unbid suits protected).

♠ 10 x   ♡ A Q x   ◊ K x x x x   ♣ K Q x

Respond 2 No Trump (14 points, all suits protected).

♠ Q x x   ♡ x x x   ◊ A J x   ♣ A K x x

Do not respond 2 No Trump. You have 14 points but no protection in Hearts. Bid 2 Clubs and await developments.

jump take-out to 3 no trump

This is a specialized bid that should be reserved for hands of the 4-3-3-3 distribution, with protection in all three unbid suits, and a point count of 16 to 18.

Partner opens with 1 Spade. You hold:

♠ J x x   ♡ A Q 10   ◊ K J x x   ♣ A Q x

You have the right type of distribution and 17 points, with all suits protected. Bid 3 No Trump.

jump take-out in a new suit

1 DIAMOND TO 2 SPADES
1 DIAMOND TO 3 CLUBS

This bid is absolutely forcing to game and strongly suggests slam possibilities. It should be made only when responder has a strong suit of his own or good support for partner's suit. Responder's point count should be at least 19.

The reason for such a high requirement is this: The jump shift announces that responder suspects there is a slam. The slam figure is 33. Responder must therefore be able to see 32 points before he talks of slam. Assuming partner has a normal minimum opening of 13 points, 13 plus 19 equals 32.

Partner opens with 1 Heart. You hold:

♠ A K Q J x x   ♡ x   ◊ A Q J x   ♣ x x

Respond 2 Spades—a slam signal despite lack of support for partner. Since your Spade suit is self-sustaining, you should value your hand as though you were the bidder. It has the value of 20 points, 17 in high cards, 2 for the singleton, and 1 for the doubleton.

Partner opens with 1 Heart. You hold:

♠ x   ♡ K J 10 x   ◊ A J x   ♣ A K x x x

Bid 3 Clubs. Since Hearts are the contemplated trumps, you should value your hand as a dummy. Your hand is worth 19 points, 16 in high cards and 3 for the singleton. It looks very much like a slam. Even if partner has only 13 points, you will have at least 32.

Partner opens with 1 Heart. You hold:

♠ A K x x   ♡ x   ◊ Q x x x   ♣ A K x x

Respond 1 Spade. Do not make a jump shift despite the high-card holding. You cannot as yet visualize a slam. The hand is worth only 18 points, valued at your own suit.

1-over-1 response

It has been observed that a response of 1 in a suit may be ambiguous. It may be the weakest holding, containing as little as 6 points, and it may be a very powerful hand, perhaps 18 points, one on which a responder is just short of the requirement for a jump shift. How can the opener tell which it is? He can't on the first round, but he will be able to tell on the second round of the auction. If responder has a weak hand, he will take no further action unless forced to do so. If he has a strong one, he will indicate it on the second lap of the race.

Partner opens with 1 Club. You hold:

♠ K 10 x x x   ♡ Q x x x   ◇ x x x   ♣ x

Respond with 1 Spade. You do not intend to bid any more, unless partner jumps to a new suit. Your hand is worth 7 points, 5 in high cards and 2 for distribution.

♠ K Q 10 x x   ♡ A J x x   ◇ x x   ♣ K x

Respond 1 Spade. You intend ultimately to contract for at least a game, but your 1 Spade bid is forcing, and when partner rebids, you will make another force on the next round. Opener will then learn that you have a good hand. Valued at Spades, your hand is worth only 15 points, 13 in high cards and 2 for distribution. It does not, therefore, approach the 19 points required for an immediate jump shift.

the response of 2 in a suit

While a response at the level of 1 does not necessarily show a good hand, a response at the level of 2 does. You should not increase a contract by bidding 2 of a new suit unless your hand contains 10 or more points. For example:

♠ x x   ♡ K x x   ◇ A J x x x   ♣ x x x

If partner opens with 1 Club, you may respond 1 Diamond, but if partner opens with 1 Spade, your hand is not good enough to increase the contract to 2 Diamonds. Your hand does not contain 10 points in high cards, and you should therefore respond 1 No Trump. You may, however, take slightly greater liberties by responding at the level of 2 if you have a six- or seven-card suit.

shall I respond with 1 of a suit or 1 no trump?

In this case, always respond with 1 of a suit. It is cheaper, and the weaker the hand, the more urgency to reply with 1 of a suit rather than 1 No Trump.

♠ K 10 9 x ♡ x x x ♢ Q J x x ♣ x x

Partner opens with 1 Club. You have 6 points in high cards and must keep the bidding open. Do so with 1 Diamond, not 1 No Trump. It permits partner to bid again at the level of 1. This might be very agreeable if he happened to be able to bid 1 Spade, which he could not have done had you responded 1 No Trump.

choice between raising partner and bidding your own suit

Which to do depends upon the strength of your hand. If your hand is valued within the minimum range—that is, 6 to 10 points—you cannot afford to make two constructive bids. You should try to bid only once. Where it is your intention to bid only once, it is much preferable to raise your partner rather than to bid your own suit. This is especially true if partner's suit happens to be a major.

If, as responder, you hold a hand that is worth 11 points or more, you should arrange to bid twice. Your hand will then be too good for a single raise. You therefore bid your own suit first and support partner later.

Partner opens with 1 Spade. You hold:

♠ A x x   ♡ x x x   ◇ x x   ♣ K Q x x x

This hand is worth 9 points in support of Spades. On the surface it appears to be worth 10, 9 in high cards and 1 for the doubleton, but it possesses the flaw of having only three trumps, so we deduct a point. Now, a 9-point hand does not justify two forward bids, so that a single raise to 2 Spades is clearly indicated.

♠ A x x x   ♡ x   ◇ K 10 x x   ♣ Q x x x

This hand is worth 12 points in support of Spades, 9 in high cards and 3 for the singleton. It is therefore not quite strong enough for a jump to 3 Spades, which would be forcing to game and requires 13 points. However, the hand is too strong for a mere raise to 2 Spades, the top limit of which is 10; so you should arrange to bid twice. This you may accomplish by a temporizing bid of 2 Diamonds. If partner rebids 2 Spades, you raise to 3, showing 11 or 12 points.

♠ A J x   ♡ x x   ◇ x x x   ♣ K Q J x x

This hand contains 11 points in support of Spades. Bid 2 Clubs and raise Spades on the next round of bidding.

responding with two suits

When responder has two suits, he must first decide whether his hand is strong enough to justify showing both. If his hand contains 11 or 12 points, he should show both suits. If it has 6 to 9 points, it is sounder to bid only once, unless partner does something sensational on his rebid.

When, as responder, you have a hand strong enough to bid both suits, show them in the logical order. That is, bid a five-card suit ahead of a four-card suit, and when both suits are of equal length, bid the higher-ranking first.

♠ A Q J x ♡ x x ◊ A 10 9 x x ♣ x x

Partner opens with 1 Heart. Your hand contains 11 points in high cards and both suits should be named. Respond 2 Diamonds, the longer suit. Do not make the mistake of bidding 1 Spade first because it is cheap. It is not necessary to keep the bidding low with hands of this strength. If you bid Spades first, partner will never ascertain your exact distribution.

With a weaker hand, such as:

♠ K J 10 x ♡ x x ◊ x x ♣ K J x x x

the proper response is 1 Spade. This hand contains only 8 points in high cards, and you cannot afford to show both suits on your own steam. Furthermore, your hand is not good enough to take out to the level of 2, so rather than bid 1 No Trump, you respond with 1 Spade, not intending to take further action, unless partner makes a very aggressive rebid.

responding when you have previously passed

When a player has previously passed, he must adopt a somewhat different attitude toward his responses. The usual forcing principles do not apply strictly. The player who has opened the bidding in third or fourth position (after his partner has passed) may let the bidding drop at almost any time. Bear in mind, therefore, when you have previously passed, any bid you make may be the final call (unless it is a jump in a new suit or a cue bid of the opponent's suit).

A jump in the same suit (1 Spade to 3 Spades) or a jump in No Trump (1 Spade to 2 No Trump) now becomes strongly invitational but not forcing. However, a jump in a new suit (1 Spade to 3 Diamonds) is forcing even when the jump comes from a passing partner.

When partner opens the bidding, after you have passed, and you feel confident you can make game in his suit, my suggestion is that you go right ahead and bid it. It follows, therefore, that, after a previous pass, a jump to 4 is stronger than a jump to 3.

It has been observed that a jump response to 2 No Trump indicates a hand containing between 13 and 15 points; it is forcing to game. After you have passed, you may jump to 2 No Trump with a little less—11 or 12 points. Such a jump is not forcing, and partner may decide whether or not to continue on the basis of the combined assets of which he will have a reasonably exact estimate. He will know, of course, that you do not have 13 to 15, else you would have opened the bidding. For example, partner in third position opens with 1 Spade. You hold:

♠ x x   ♡ K J x   ◇ A Q x x   ♣ J 10 x x

Respond 2 No Trump ('11 points)'; partner should pass if he opened a minimum hand.

A jump in a new suit, after a previous pass, is forcing.

Partner in third position opens with 1 Club. You hold:

♠ K Q J 9 x   ♡ x   ◊ Q 10 x   ♣ K J x x

Respond 2 Spades.

quiz no. 2: responses

[(Answers follow this quiz)]

1. Partner bids 1 Spade. You hold:

♠ x x x x   ♥ A x x   ♦ x x x   ♣ x x x

What is your response?

2. Partner bids 1 Spade. You hold:

♠ K J x x x   ♥ x x x   ♦ x x   ♣ K x x x

What is your response?

3. Partner bids 1 Spade. You hold:

♠ x x x   ♥ K Q x   ♦ K x x   ♣ A Q x x

What is your response?

4. Partner bids 1 Heart. You hold:

♠ K J x   ♥ J x x   ♦ A Q x x   ♣ A Q x

What is your response?

5. Partner bids 1 Heart. You hold:
   ♠ xx ♡ Kxxx ◇ KQJx ♣ J10x
   What is your response?

6. Partner bids 1 Heart. You hold:
   ♠ AJ10x ♡ Jxxx ◇ xx ♣ xxx
   What is your response?

7. Partner bids 1 No Trump. You hold:
   ♠ QJxxxxx ♡ x ◇ Qxxx ♣ x
   What is your response?

8. Partner bids 1 Club. You hold:
   ♠ Axx ♡ KJxx ◇ Axxx ♣ xx
   What is your response?

9. Partner bids 1 Club. You hold:
   ♠ KJx ♡ KQx ◇ A10xx ♣ Axx
   What is your response?

10. Partner bids 1 Club. You hold:
    ♠ none ♡ KJx ◇ AQ10xx ♣ Axxxx
    What is your response?

11. Partner opens with 2 Hearts. You hold:
    ♠ QJ10xx ♡ xxx ◇ xx ♣ Axx
    What is your response?

12. Partner opens with 2 Spades. You hold:
♠ J 9 x x   ♡ A x x   ◇ K x   ♣ x x x x
What is your response?

13. Partner opens with 2 Hearts. You hold:
♠ Q 10 x x x   ♡ x   ◇ x x x   ♣ x x x x
What is your response?

14. Partner opens with 2 Hearts. You hold:
♠ K x x   ♡ x x   ◇ K x x x   ♣ K x x x
What is your response?

15. Partner opens with 2 Spades. You hold:
♠ x   ♡ K 10 9 x x x   ◇ x x x   ♣ x x x
What is your response?

16. Partner opens with 2 Hearts. You hold:
♠ x x   ♡ Q x x   ◇ K Q x   ♣ 10 x x x x
What is your response?

17. Partner opens with 2 Hearts. You hold:
♠ A Q x x   ♡ x x   ◇ K J 10 x   ♣ x x x x
What is your response?

18. Partner opens with 2 Spades. You hold:
♠ x   ♡ x x   ◇ Q J 9 x x x x   ♣ Q x x
What is your response?

answers to quiz no. 2

1. Pass. This hand contains only 4 points and no distributional features. Therefore, it does not have sufficient values to keep the bidding alive.

2. Bid 2 Spades. Do not get excited because of that fifth trump. The hand would be almost as good without it. This hand contains only 8 points in support of a Spade bid, 7 points in high cards and 1 point for the doubleton Diamond.

3. 2 No Trump, an exact descriptive bid. This hand has all unbid suits protected and a point count of 14; in other words, the equal of an opening bid. Nothing is to be gained by temporizing with an indirect bid of 2 Clubs.

4. 3 No Trump. You have just the right distribution and honor strength (17 points). A 2 No Trump response would be highly improper.

5. 2 Diamonds. An indirect bid is necessary because the hand is too good for a single raise and not good enough for a raise to 3 Hearts. You will support Hearts on the next round.

6. 2 Hearts, not 1 Spade. You cannot afford to do both and you should make the more important bid, which is a raise of partner's major suit.

7. 4 Spades. Game is sure, but a slam is entirely out of the question. Such a pre-emptive response describes a hand which is not rich in high cards.

8. 1 Heart. This hand contains only 12 points and is therefore fractionally short of the high-card requirement for a 2 No Trump response. It is preferable to show the major suit first and then try No Trump later. A response of 1 Diamond would also be accepted.

9. 3 No Trump, a balanced hand with a point count of 17, an exact descriptive bid which is preferable to a temporizing bid of 1 Diamond. Take only half credit if your answer was 1 Diamond.

10. 2 Diamonds, a jump shift suggesting slam possibilities. Your good trump fit and controls justified such optimism.

11. 2 Spades. You have 7 points in high cards and a good five-card suit. This is enough to make a positive response, and you do so by showing your suit at the cheapest level.

12. Bid 3 Spades. When responding to a 2 bid, the best policy is to announce support in your partner's suit. This does not deny outside values which you will show on later rounds of bidding.

13. Bid 2 No Trump. Your first duty is to advise partner that you do not hold 7 points in support of his 2 bid. Here you make the negative response of 2 No Trump, which says: "Partner, I have no encouraging values. Be guided accordingly."

14. 3 No Trump. With 8 or 9 points in high cards divided in two or more suits and no particularly biddable suit, you skip the negative 2 No Trump response and respond 3 No Trump. Here you hold 9 points divided in three suits and therefore have the ideal holding for such a call.

15. 2 No Trump. Despite the possession of your long and fairly good Heart suit, your first duty is to announce the lack of high-card values by making the denial bid of 2 No Trump. At the next opportunity you may show the Heart suit. This should tell partner exactly what kind of hand you hold.

16. Bid 3 Hearts. Three to a queen is ample trump support, particularly in response to an opening 2 bid where the suit is almost invariably a good one. You hold 7 points in high cards and 1 point by virtue of the doubleton, and in addition the value of the Queen of Hearts is enhanced. Do not make the mistake of responding 3 Clubs on a suit that is not biddable despite its being five cards long.

17. 2 Spades. You have 10 points and a biddable Spade suit, which entitles you to make a forward bid.

18. 2 No Trump. With only 5 points in high cards and no fit for partner's bid suit, you are forced to make a negative response. When next you get the opportunity to bid, you will show the Diamond suit. This will advise partner that you have a Diamond suit but not enough values for a positive response.

rebids by opener

The action taken by the opening bidder the second time around is usually the most vital of the auction. Unless the opener inaugurated proceedings with a certain number of No Trump, the opening bid is always vague and ambiguous. It may be light, moderate, or strong. The second bid should tell the story and classify the hand as to strength. For example:

♠ A K Q x x   ♡ K x x   ◇ A 10 x   ♣ J x

You open with 1 Spade; partner responds 2 Clubs. Your rebid should be 2 No Trump to show the strength of your hand. A rebid of 2 Spades to show a good suit would be improper since such a rebid describes a rebiddable suit with only a mediocre hand, ranging between 13 and 16 points. The following table may be used to help you determine what type of rebid you may make as opener:

13 to 16 points:
Your hand is in the minimum range. You may or may not bid again, unless partner's response is forcing.

17 to 18 points:

You have a good hand and you are in a position to make a constructive rebid. Avoid making any rebid which your partner may construe as discouraging.

19 to 21 points:

You have a very good hand. This is in the jump rebid range. Either jump in No Trump or jump in your own suit, or in partner's suit.

22 and up:

This is a super hand. Of course, you are going to game. You should personally see to that by making a jump shift which partner is not permitted to pass and which is forcing to game.

rebids when partner has given you a single raise

1 HEART TO 2 HEARTS

When partner raises your suit, add an additional point for the fifth trump and 2 additional points for the sixth and each subsequent trump. For example:

♠ A K x x x ♡ A Q x ◇ x x ♣ x x

You open with 1 Spade; partner raises you to 2 Spades. The original valuation of your hand was 15 points, 13 in high cards and 1 for each doubleton. Now that partner has supported Spades, you add 1 point for the fifth Spade and 2 points for the sixth, so that your hand, after the raise, has an adjusted value of 18 points. If partner has 8 points, you will have enough for game.

Since partner's raise may be rather light, caution is indicated. Partner's raise is limited to 6 to 10 points. Therefore, if you have opened with 13 or 14 points, game is not to be considered. With 15, it would be highly doubtful, and with 16, if partner's raise was maximum, you would have the necessary 26 for game.

You open with 1 Heart; partner raises to 2. You hold:

♠ x x ♡ A K x x x ◇ Q x x ♣ A x x

Pass. Your hand had an original valuation of 14 points. Now that partner has raised, you add 1 point for the fifth Heart, giving you an adjusted valuation of 15 points. You see, therefore, there is little hope for game. Even if partner has the limit of 10 points, you will not have the necessary 26.

You open with 1 Heart; partner raises to 2. You hold:

♠ A K x ♡ A K Q x x ◇ J x x x ♣ x

Bid 4 Hearts. Your hand had an original valuation of 19 points. Since partner has supported Hearts, you add 1 point for the fifth card of that suit, giving your hand an adjusted valuation of 20 points. Even if partner has raised with only 6 points, you will have enough for game.

♠ A 10 x ♡ A K x x ◇ A Q 10 x ♣ x x

Bid 3 Diamonds. You have 17 points in high cards, and if partner's raise contains 9, there should be a play for game either at Hearts or at No Trump. Therefore, you must try again.

rebids when partner responds 1 no trump

When your partner responds with 1 No Trump and you have a balanced hand yourself—that is, one distributed:

4-3-3-3
4-3-3-2
5-3-3-2

you must stick to No Trump. Raise if you can, pass if you are unable to raise, but don't rebid your suit or show another suit. *The best place to play an indifferent hand is 1 No Trump.* In this position it is relatively easy to compute the partnership assets, for you know that your partner has between 6 and 9 points. If your hand is suitable for No Trump and you know that the partnership has 26 points, go to 3 No Trump. If the partnership assets may or may not reach 26 points, go to 2 No Trump, offering partner his chance to proceed if he has 8 or 9 rather than 6 or 7.

If you know that it is impossible for your partnership to have 26 points, don't bid any more, unless you have an unbalanced hand. Remember, when No Trump bids are contemplated, you do not count distributional values, just high cards.

♠ K Q x ♡ x x ◇ A K 10 x x ♣ Q x x

Pass. You have 14 points, and even if partner has 9, you will be far removed from the 26 necessary to make game. Since your hand is of the No Trump family, you must not rebid your suit.

♠ A K J x   ♡ x x x   ◇ A Q J x   ♣ x x

Pass. You have 15 points, no hope for game, even if partner has 9. You have a balanced hand, so the other suit should not be mentioned.

♠ A x   ♡ A K 10 x   ◇ A x x x   ♣ K x x

Bid 2 No Trump. You have 18 points. If partner has 6 or 7, he will pass. If he has 8 or 9, you will have the required values for a game contract and he should bid it.

♠ A J x   ♡ A K 10 x   ◇ K Q   ♣ A x x x

Bid 3 No Trump. You have 21 points. Partner is known to have at least 6 points, so that your combined assets are more than the 26 required for game.

♠ x x x   ♡ A Q x x x x   ◇ x   ♣ A x x

Bid 2 Hearts. This is a minimum hand but is unsuitable for No Trump. The six-card major should be rebid.

♠ K x x   ♡ A K 10 9 x x   ◇ x   ♣ A Q x

Your hand had an original value of 18 points. (Where your suit is self-sustaining, you may revalue it as though partner had supported it. Accordingly, 3 points are added, 1 for the fifth and 2 for the sixth trump. This gives your hand the value of 21 points.) Bid 3 Hearts.

If your hand is a bit stronger, 22 rebid points or more, you should bid game directly, unless you are able to make a jump shift.

♠ K Q 10 x x ♡ A Q 10 x x ◇ x ♣ A Q

You have opened with 1 Spade; partner responds
1 No Trump. With this fine hand you do not choose
to play for less than game, and partner would very
likely pass a rebid of 2 Hearts. Bid 3 Hearts.

rebid when responder bids 1 of a suit

When responder makes a 1-over-1 take-out, opener
must indicate on his rebid the approximate nature
of his hand. If he has a minimum hand, he indicates
it in one of three ways:

1. By a rebid of 1 No Trump.
2. By a rebid of his own suit.
3. By naming a new suit at the level of 1.

Opener, holding a minimum hand, may also rebid
a new suit at the level of 2 if it is the cheapest possible
range at which his two-suiter can be shown. For
example:

You open with 1 Heart; partner responds with 1
Spade.

♠ x x x ♡ A Q J x ◇ K x x x ♣ A x x

Rebid 1 No Trump, showing a minimum hand of
the balanced type.

♠ x ♡ A K J x x x ◇ K x x ♣ x x x

Rebid 2 Hearts, showing a minimum hand of the
suit type.

♠ x x ♡ K Q 10 x x ◇ A Q x x x ♣ x

Rebid 2 Diamonds. This is a two-suiter and the
cheapest level at which you are able to show your
second suit.

You open with 1 Club; partner responds with 1 Diamond.

♠ xx   ♡ AKxx   ◊ xxx   ♣ AQxx

Rebid 1 Heart. Showing a new suit at the level of 1 requires no additional values.

raising partner from 1 to 2

This shows that opener had a little bit more than a minimum. Opener now revalues his hand as though it were a dummy for his partner; and if he has a little more than 13, he may raise, provided he has normal trump support.

♠ Axxx   ♡ AKJxx   ◊ xx   ♣ xx

You open with 1 Heart; partner responds 1 Spade. Raise to 2 Spades. Valued as a dummy, your hand has 14 points, 12 in high cards and 1 for each doubleton.

♠ xx   ♡ Axx   ◊ AKJxx   ♣ xxx

You open with 1 Diamond; partner responds 1 Heart. With this hand a raise should not be given. It has the valuation of 13 points if played at Diamonds and only 12 points in support of Hearts. A rebid of 2 Diamonds is recommended.

♠ Ax   ♡ Qxx   ◊ AJxxx   ♣ Qxx

You open with 1 Diamond; partner bids 1 Heart. Rebid 1 No Trump. You have a minimum hand.

♠ A 10xx ♡ x ◇ xxxx ♣ A K J x

You open with 1 Club; partner responds 1 Spade.
A raise to 2 Spades is justified. You have 12 points
in high cards and 3 for the singleton; 15 points are
ample for a single raise in partner's suit.

raising responder from 1 to 3

In order to raise responder from 1 to 3, opener
should have 17 to 19 points, but his holding must include at least four trumps.

♠ Axxx ♡ KQxx ◇ x ♣ AQxx

You open with 1 Club; partner responds 1 Spade.
Rebid 3 Spades. Your hand has a value of 18 points
in support of Spades, 15 in high cards and 3 for the
singleton.

This jump to 3 Spades is not forcing. If partner's 1
Spade bid consisted of barely 6 points, he may exercise
his option to pass.

♠ AJxx ♡ Kx ◇ xx ♣ AKxxx

You open with 1 Club; partner responds 1 Spade.
Rebid 3 Spades. Your hand is worth 17 points in support of Spades, and since your trump support is more
than adequate, that bid is justified.

raising responder from 1 to 4

This raise shows a hand which contains 19 to 21
points, and therefore is good enough to make game,

even if partner's response was a rock-bottom minimum. This is by no means a "shut-out" bid.

♠ K Q x x   ♥ A J x   ♦ x   ♣ A K x x x

You open with 1 Club; partner responds 1 Spade. Bid 4 Spades. Your hand has the value of 20 points in support of Spades and you do not wish to take the risk that partner will pass a raise to 3 Spades if he has been sporting enough to respond with 1 Spade, holding:

♠ J x x x x   ♥ K x x   ♦ J x x   ♣ x x

jump rebid to 2 no trump

This rebid describes a hand suitable for No Trump and containing 19 or 20 points.

Keep your eye on the figure 26 for the combined partnership assets necessary to produce game. If you are sure you have them, contract for game. If there is some slight doubt, invite partner to undertake a game contract.

The jump rebid to 2 No Trump is not forcing; responder may quit if his response is based on only 6 points. An illustration:

♠ J x   ♥ A Q x   ♦ K Q J x   ♣ A Q x x

You open with 1 Diamond; partner responds 1 Spade. You have 19 points in high cards. It will take about 7 points in partner's hand to reach the required 26. But he may not have as many as 7. He may have only 6 or possibly only 5 in high cards, so that you are not quite in a position to contract for game. However, by jumping to 2 No Trump you announce to partner that you are on the verge of a game at No Trump, for which he should contract if he has anything more than 6 points. In other words, opener announces a holding of about 19 or 20 points.

It is a common error for opener to jump to 2 No Trump on the second round merely because he has more than his opening bid. Try to avoid it.

jump rebid to 3 no trump

This rebid is made on a hand which is somewhat stronger than the one on which a rebid of 2 No Trump is recommended; in other words, about 21 or 22 points. Even if partner has a shaded response—that is, 5 or 6 points—you may expect to make game.

♠ Q x   ♡ A K 10   ◇ A Q J x x   ♣ A J x

You open with 1 Diamond; partner responds 1 Spade. Rebid 3 No Trump. You have 21 points, which should provide a good play for game even if partner has less than 6.

jump rebid in opener's suit

OPENER	RESPONDER
1 ♡	1 ♠
3 ♡	

(19 to 21 points in rebid valuation)

Such a jump rebid is not forcing. It strongly urges responder to bid again, but responder may pass if his response was made with less than normal strength and no particular distributional advantages. The jump rebid shows a very fine trump suit which requires very little trump support from partner (two small trumps are sufficient), and some additional high-card values.

♠ K x   ♡ A K 10 9 x x   ◇ A Q x   ♣ x x

You open with 1 Heart; partner responds 1 Spade. Rebid 3 Hearts. Your hand had an original value of 18 points. Since your suit is self-sustaining, you may revalue it as though partner had supported it; the addition of 1 point for the fifth trump and 2 points for the sixth trump gives your hand a rebid value of 21 points, which justifies the jump.

♠ x   ♡ A K Q J x x   ◇ x x x   ♣ K x x

You open with 1 Heart; partner responds 1 Spade. Do not jump to 3 Hearts. Even though you hold a very fine trump suit, your hand does not total enough to meet the requirement. Rebid 2 Hearts, and if partner takes any further action, your next bid should be 4 Hearts.

jump rebid to 4 of opener's suit

OPENER	RESPONDER
1 ♡	1 ♠
4 ♡	

(22 to 23 points)

This bid describes a hand that can win between 8 and 9 tricks by itself.

♠ K x ♡ A K Q x x x x ◇ A x ♣ x x

You can win about nine tricks yourself and should
not incur the risk of having partner pass you short
of game. This is by no means a "shut-out" bid.

jump shift by opening bidder

OPENER	RESPONDER
1 ♡	1 ♠
3 ◇	

(22 points and up)

This is the only way in which opener can force
responder to bid again. This bid is forcing to game,
and responder may not pass, even if he regrets having
responded at all.

♠ J x ♡ A K Q 10 x ◇ x ♣ A K Q x x

You open with 1 Heart; partner responds with 1
Spade. Even if partner has less than a normal Spade
response, you wish to insist upon a game contract, so
you must rebid 3 Clubs, which is forcing to game. A
mere rebid of 2 Clubs could be dropped by responder.

♠ x ♡ K x x x ◇ A K J 10 x ♣ A K J

You open with 1 Diamond; partner responds 1
Heart. A jump to 3 Hearts is out of the question.
Partner might have made a sporting response with
a King and a Queen, or perhaps a couple of Queens,
in which case he would surely drop the bidding. The
proper rebid is a jump in a new suit, forcing to game.

You have no new suit, to be sure, but for the purpose of executing a jump shift, you may improvise one, and the proper rebid is 3 Clubs (intending all the time to support Hearts on the next round).

rebid by opener when responder bids 2 of a new suit

Whenever the opening bidder's second bid is at the range of 3, he should have a very strong hand. For example:

OPENER	RESPONDER
1 ♡	2 ◊
3 ♣	

Opener advertises a hand of considerable strength. When opener's rebid is 2 No Trump, even though it is not a jump, he promises a good hand. For example:

OPENER	RESPONDER
1 ♡	2 ◊
2 NT	

Opener promises that he has at least 16 points in high cards.

♠ A x   ♡ A K J x x   ◊ K J x   ♣ Q x x

You open with 1 Heart; partner responds 2 Clubs. Rebid 2 No Trump. You have a point count of 18 in high cards. Don't make the mistake of rebidding

2 Hearts, which would describe a hand in the minimum range (13 to 16).

♠ x x   ♡ A K J x x   ◇ Q x x   ♣ K x x

You open with 1 Heart; partner responds 2 Clubs. You have trump support but no additional values to justify a raise to 3 Clubs. You must be content, therefore, with a rebid of 2 Hearts. Where the question is: *Shall I raise partner or rebid my suit? The answer is: Raise partner if you wish to take the aggressive step; rebid your suit if you do not wish to sound too encouraging.*

quiz no. 3: rebids by opener

(Answers follow this quiz).

1. As South you hold:

   ♠ A 10 x ♡ A K Q x x ◇ K x x ♣ J x

   The bidding has proceeded:

South	West	North	East
1 ♡	P	2 ♣	P
?			

   What is your rebid?

2. You open with 1 Spade; partner raises to 2. You hold:

   ♠ A K x x x ♡ Q x x ◇ x x ♣ A x x

   What is your rebid?

3. You open with 1 Spade; partner raises to 2. You hold:

   ♠ A K x x x ♡ A J x ◇ K J x ♣ x x

   What is your rebid?

4. As South you hold:

♠ A K Q x x ♥ x ♦ A K J ♣ x x x x

You open with 1 Spade; partner raises to 2. What is your rebid?

5. As South you hold:

♠ A Q 10 x ♥ A K x x ♦ A 10 x ♣ x x

You open with 1 Spade; partner raises to 2. What is your rebid?

6. You open with 1 Heart; partner responds 1 No Trump. You hold:

♠ x x ♥ A K 10 x x ♦ K Q x ♣ Q x x

What is your rebid?

7. You open with 1 Heart; partner responds 1 No Trump. You hold:

♠ x x x ♥ A Q J x ♦ A K J x ♣ x x

What do you do?

8. You open with 1 Spade; partner bids 1 No Trump. You hold:

♠ A K 10 x ♥ A J x ♦ A x x x ♣ K Q

What is your rebid?

9. You open with 1 Spade; partner responds 1 No Trump. You hold:

♠ A K x x x ♥ x ♦ A Q J x ♣ x x x

What is your rebid?

10. You open with 1 Spade; partner responds 1 No Trump. You hold:

♠ A Q x x x x ♡ x ◇ x x x ♣ A x x

What is your rebid?

11. You open with 1 Spade; partner responds 1 No Trump. You hold:

♠ K Q J x x ♡ K Q 10 x x ◇ A Q ♣ x

What is your rebid?

12. You open with 1 Heart; partner responds 1 No Trump. You hold:

♠ x ♡ A Q x x x ◇ K Q 10 x x ♣ x x

What is your rebid?

13. You open with 1 Club; partner responds 1 Heart. You hold:

♠ A J x x ♡ x x ◇ x x x ♣ A K x x

What is your rebid?

14. You open with 1 Diamond; partner responds 1 Heart. You hold:

♠ x ♡ A x x ◇ A K J x x ♣ x x x x

What is your rebid?

15. You open with 1 Diamond; partner responds 1 Spade. You hold:

♠ A 10 x x ♡ x x ◇ A K J x ♣ J 10 x

What is your rebid?

16. You open with 1 Club; partner responds 1 Spade. You hold:

    ♠ A 10 x x ♡ x x ◇ K x ♣ A K J x x

What is your rebid?

17. You open with 1 Club; partner responds 1 Spade. You hold:

    ♠ K Q 10 x ♡ x x ◇ A Q J ♣ A K Q x

What is your rebid?

18. You open with 1 Diamond; partner responds 1 Spade. You hold:

    ♠ Q x ♡ K J x ◇ A K J x ♣ A J x x

What is your rebid?

19. You open with 1 Diamond; partner responds 1 Spade. You hold:

    ♠ x x ♡ A x x ◇ A K x x ♣ A x x x

What is your rebid?

20. You open with 1 Diamond; partner responds 1 Spade. You hold:

    ♠ J x ♡ A Q 10 ◇ A Q 10 x x ♣ A K J

What is your rebid?

21. You open with 1 Heart; partner responds 1 Spade. You hold:

    ♠ K x ♡ A K Q x x x x ◇ A x ♣ J x

What is your rebid?

22. You open with 1 Diamond; partner responds 1 Spade. You hold:

♠ K x x x   ♡ x   ◇ A K J x x   ♣ A K x

What is your rebid?

23. You open with 1 Spade; partner bids 2 Hearts. You hold:

♠ A Q 10 x x   ♡ x   ◇ A Q 10 x x   ♣ x x

What is your rebid?

24. You open with 1 Diamond; partner responds 2 Clubs. You hold:

♠ A x x   ♡ K Q x   ◇ A J 10 x x   ♣ x x

What is your rebid?

answers to quiz no. 3

1. Your rebid should be 2 No Trump to show the strength of your hand. Here you have a choice between showing a strong suit and a strong hand. In all these cases where you cannot do both, it is better to show a strong hand. A rebid of 2 Hearts would be improper since such a call describes a rebiddable suit with only a mediocre hand. A minimum rebid should never be made with a hand worth more than 16 points.

2. You have opened on a hand which is valued at 14 points, which places it in the minimum category. Partner has made a minimum response, which, at best, leaves you somewhat short of the total necessary for game. Therefore, a pass is indicated.

3. When you opened the bidding, your holding was valued at 17 points, 16 in high cards and 1 for the doubleton. When partner has supported your suit, you may add 1 point for the value of the fifth Spade, making your total 18 points. Partner's raise may be anywhere from 6 to 10 points, bringing your total to a minimum of 24 points. This should render a contract of 3 Spades safe. If partner has raised on more than minimum values, he will take you to game.

4. You have opened with a point count of 19 points, 17 in high cards and 2 by virtue of the singleton. When partner supports your suit, you may add 1 point for the fifth Spade, bringing your total to 20 points. Partner has promised at least 6 points when he raised your suit. Therefore, the combined total is a minimum of 26 points, which warrants your contracting for game immediately. Bid 4 Spades.

5. 3 Hearts. Since you have opened a hand with 17 points, game is not impossible, as partner's response may total anywhere from 6 to 10 points. The change of suit, since partner has raised your suit, is forcing for one round. It is possible that partner has a better Heart holding than Spades, in which case he might raise you to game in Hearts. If partner is able to bid 3 No Trump, you should be delighted to pass. If partner can do no more than return to 3 Spades, you will have done your duty and can now pass.

6. Pass. You have 14 points, and even if partner has the top limit for his No Trump call, which is 9 points, you will be far removed from the 26 necessary to make game. Since your hand is of the No Trump family, you must not rebid your suit. Pass and play for seven rather than eight tricks.

7. Partner's No Trump response shows a hand which contains 6 to 9 points. You have 15; therefore, you are below the necessary 26 needed for game. Your 4-4-3-2 distribution is in the No Trump family, so your other suit should not be mentioned. Again play for seven tricks rather than eight.

8. Bid 3 No Trump. You have opened with 21 points and partner has announced at least 6 points, which brings the combined total to a minimum of 27, which is more than enough to warrant contracting for game.

9. Bid 2 Diamonds. You have no prospect of going to game. But this is an unbalanced hand and not in the No Trump family and may, therefore, play better at a suit. The proper rebid is 2 Diamonds, not 2 Spades. The 2 Diamond bid permits partner to return to 2 Spades and affords him two chances to find the proper parking place.

10. Bid 2 Spades. This is a minimum hand but is unsuitable for play at No Trump, and the six-card major suit should be rebid.

11. Bid 3 Hearts. This jump shift in the new suit is forcing to game. With this fine hand you should not choose to play for less than game. With a partner who can respond at all, a play for game must be available in either one of your suits or No Trump. Do not bid

2 Hearts, since partner would very likely pass that call.

12. Since game is hopeless in view of partner's mild response and the fact that you have opened a minimum hand, your rebid is 2 Diamonds, which shows no great strength but merely gives partner the opportunity to show his preference for either one of your suits.

13. Bid 1 Spade. Showing a new suit at the level of 1 requires no additional values. You opened with a Club to prepare the way for the indicated rebid.

14. Your hand contains 14 points in support of partner's bid suit, 12 in high cards but only 2 by way of distribution. However, on all hands from 14 to 16 points, where you are able to raise partner's suit it is advisable to do so rather than rebid your own suit. If your hand had only 13 points, it would be better to show your minimum by rebidding your own suit.

15. Bid 2 Spades. You have 13 points in high cards and 1 point for the doubleton, which brings your total to 14 points, and therefore you are justified in raising partner's suit bid once.

16. 3 Spades. You have 17 points in support of a Spade contract, 15 in high cards and 1 for each doubleton. The requirement for the jump raise of partner's bid suit is a hand containing good trump support and 17 to 19 points in high cards and distribution.

17. Four Spades. You have 21 points in high cards and 1 for the doubleton, which brings your total to

22. You cannot risk a possible pass by partner, who may have a subnormal response. Bid 4 Spades directly, which, incidentally, is a mild try for slam.

18. You have 19 points and all unmentioned suits safely stopped. Rebid 2 No Trump, which exactly describes your holding. If partner has exactly 6 points, he may pass, for then the play for game will be doubtful. If he has any more, he should, of course, accept your strong invitation.

19. Despite the possession of four honor tricks, your hand is still in the minimum range since it totals only 15 points in high cards. Do not make the mistake of jumping to 2 No Trump, which would describe a holding of 19 points in high cards. Bid 1 No Trump. If partner cannot bid again, you need not fear the loss of a game.

20. You have 21 points and a 5-3-3-2 distribution, with all suits safely accounted for. Rebid 3 No Trump. That bid describes your holding in one shot.

21. 4 Hearts. You have opened a hand with 20 points and in addition have a suit which needs no support from partner, and you have the King of the suit in which partner has responded. Do not risk a 3 Heart bid, which partner might conceivably pass, since any hand on which partner might have made his response should be good enough to produce the play for game. It should be observed that this is in no way a sign off, but, on the contrary, urges partner to continue further if he has any attractive values above the minimum of 6 points.

22. 3 Clubs. Your hand is worth 22 points in support of a Spade contract and, combined with partner's holding, assures you of sufficient values to insist upon a game contract. With your controls and the singleton Heart, there is a strong likelihood of a slam. Therefore, a 4 Spade bid would not quite describe your hand. You will, of course, raise Spades when partner bids again.

23. 2 Spades. You may not bid 3 Diamonds, since you opened a hand valued at 15 points which is still in the minimum range. If partner prefers Spades, he will have to express his preference at the level of 3. In order to bid 3 Diamonds over 2 Hearts, your hand would have to be considerably better. Of course, if partner had responded 2 Clubs to your 1 Spade bid, you would naturally respond 2 Diamonds, since here partner could go back to 2 Spades if he so desired.

24. 2 Diamonds. Do not make the mistake of rebidding 2 No Trump because you have the unbid suits stopped. Your hand is still in the minimum range, as you have opened with 14 points in high cards, and a rebid of 2 No Trump over partner's bid would show a hand containing 16 to 18 points.

rebids by responder

Whenever responder's original reply has been in-definite in its nature, as, for example, when he has made a take-out to 1 of a suit, it usually devolves upon him, on the second round of bidding, to make it clear whether he has a weak, moderate, or strong hand. The following table may be used as a fairly accurate guide to the kind of bids responder should make:

6 to 10 points:
Your hand is minimum and you should make a mild response. With 6 or 7 points, do not bid again unless forced to. With 8 or 9 points, bid once more if partner coaxes you to.

10 to 13 points:
You have a good hand. It is worth two bids.

13 to 16 points:
You have a very good hand and must see to it that you reach game. (*An opening bid,*

facing an opening bid, generally produces a game.) Either bid game directly or continue to make forcing responses (new suits) until you reach a satisfactory game contract.

16 to 19 points: You have a very powerful hand. You must show that you have more than an opening bid. You may do this by jumping to 3 No Trump, or by bidding a suit and then making a big jump the next round.

19 and up: This hand will produce a slam unless partner has a minimum. You must therefore give the immediate slam signal by jumping in a new suit.

examples of rebids by responder

♠ A Q J x x ♡ J x x ◊ x x ♣ K Q x

Partner opens with 1 Heart; you respond 1 Spade. You have learned from partner's rebid that he has a good Heart suit for which you now have adequate support. Your hand is equal to an opening bid (13 points). It faces an opening bid, so there should be game; and since you have a convenient contract (Hearts), you should bid a game in Hearts without further ado.

♠ x x ♡ A K x x x ◊ K x x ♣ J 10 x

Partner opens with 1 Spade; you respond 2 Hearts; partner rebids 2 Spades. You have 11 points in high cards, plus a five-card suit which is almost an opening bid. Even though partner has announced near minimum values by rebidding his own suit, you should try once more. Bid 2 No Trump. Remember, partner may have 15 points, which would be enough.

♠ K x x   ♡ A K J x   ◊ 10 x x   ♣ Q x x

Partner opens with 1 Club; you respond 1 Heart. Partner's rebid is 1 No Trump, showing a balanced hand of only moderate strength. You have 13 points, and partner, to open on a balanced hand, must have at least 13—so the required 26 points are there. Bid 3 No Trump.

♠ J x x   ♡ A K x x   ◊ K x x   ♣ 10 x x

Partner opens with 1 Club; you respond 1 Heart. Partner rebids 1 No Trump. You cannot promise a game if partner has a minimum, since your hand totals only 11 points in high cards, but there is still hope. If partner has 15 points, the necessary 26 will be there. You raise to 2 No Trump, which partner will pass if he has a minimum.

rebids by responder who has previously given a single raise

OPENER	RESPONDER
1 ♠	2 ♠
3 ♠ ?	

In this case responder has given a single raise and opener has made another bid. What message is opener attempting to get across? Something like this: "Partner, at this time I do not know whether you have a weak raise or a good one. If you have a good one, I'd like to go to game. If not, pass. It's up to you." If you have raised on 6 or 7 points, pass. If you have raised on 8, 9, or 10 points, bid game.

The bidding has proceeded:

OPENER	RESPONDER
1 ♡	2 ♡
3 ♡	

As responder you hold:

♠ xx ♡ Qxxx ◊ Kxx ♣ Axxx

Bid 4 Hearts. You have a good raise—10 points in support of Hearts.

♠ xx ♡ Qxxx ◊ xxx ♣ Kxxx

Pass. This is a weak raise, containing about 6 points in support of Hearts.

rebid when opener raises responder's suit

OPENER	RESPONDER
1 ◊	1 ♠
2 ♠	

Responder's problems in this situation can be solved with ease if he will bear in mind that 26 points in the combined hands are required for game.

In this case he need not have as good as an opening bid, since opener, by raising the responder, has shown that he has more than a minimum opening bid. Responder may therefore see a chance for game even if he has somewhat less than an opening bid. For example:

♠ x x x   ♡ A K J x x   ♢ J x x   ♣ x x

Partner opens with 1 Diamond; you bid 1 Heart. Opener raises to 2 Hearts. Your hand had an original valuation of 10 points 9 in high cards and 1 for the doubleton; and since Hearts have been supported, you may add an additional point for the value of the fifth Heart, which brings your hand to 11 points. Partner is known to have at least 14, since he has opened the bidding and raised you. Bid 3 Hearts. If partner has any additional value at all, he should go to game. If he raised your Heart bid with a hand that was worth only 13 or 14 points, he should be content to drop the bidding at 3.

♠ x x   ♡ A Q 10 x x   ♢ J x x   ♣ K J x

In the same bidding sequence you should go to 4 Hearts with this hand. You have an opening bid, particularly since Hearts have been supported, opposite an opening bid, and you have found the correct contract.

rebids by responder after he has responded 1 no trump

OPENER	RESPONDER
1 ♡	1 NT
2 NT	

What is opener trying to convey by his 2 No Trump bid? Simply this: He knows that responder, for his 1 No Trump bid, has 6, 7, 8, or 9 points. He is saying,

"There may or may not be game. If your 1 No Trump is in the lower bracket, 6 or 7, we probably have no game, but if it is in the upper bracket—that is, 8 or 9—game is very likely."

You are responder. The bidding has proceeded:

OPENER	RESPONDER
1 ♡	1 NT
2 NT	?

1. ♠ Q x x ♡ x x ♦ A 10 x x ♣ x x x x

2. ♠ Q x x ♡ 10 x x ♦ K x x x ♣ K x x x

With No. 1 you should pass. You have only 6 points, the minimum No Trump response. With No. 2 you should bid 3 No Trump. You have 8 points. Partner is asking you to continue if you are in the upper bracket.

responder shows a preference

When opener has shown two suits, responder must select that trump which will best serve the partnership interest, not the one he personally likes better. In making the choice, numerical superiority is the deciding factor; three small trumps are superior to A-K alone. Many players will select the doubleton A-K as trump, not realizing that those two cards will be winners even though the other suit is selected as trump.

Sometimes it is necessary for responder to increase the contract with a mediocre hand in order to arrive at the best trump. For example:

♠ Q x ♡ 10 x x ♦ J x x x ♣ K J x x

Opener bids 1 Heart; you respond 1 No Trump; opener bids 2 Spades. You should return to 3 Hearts. The partnership has eight Hearts as against only six Spades. Partner has shown five Hearts and four Spades.

as responder, must I speak again?

The showing of a new suit forces only the player who has opened the bidding. All other players at the table may check out at any time it suits their taste to do so.

When partner jumps in a new suit, you must speak again. When you are the responder, you need not bid again even when opener jumps, if the jump happens to be in the same suit (that is, a suit previously mentioned by either of you). If you are responder, you need not bid again if opener jumps in No Trump.

♠ x x x ♡ J x x x ◇ K Q 10 x x ♣ x

Partner opens with 1 Club; you respond 1 Diamond.

1. If partner's rebid is 1 Spade, you should pass. Spades suit you better than Clubs, and the new suit does not force you because you are not the opener.

2. If partner's rebid is 2 No Trump, you should not speak again. If 6 points are all partner needs, he should jump to 3 No Trump himself, for he knows you have at least that much.

3. If partner's rebid is 3 Clubs or 3 Diamonds, you should pass. He is jumping in a suit previously bid by one of you.

4. If partner's rebid is 2 Hearts, a jump in a new

suit, you would not be permitted to pass. You should then bid 3 Hearts. If partner's rebid is 2 Spades, you do not raise with only three trumps, since opener is presumed to have only four Spades. Your best bet is to rebid Diamonds and hope for the best.

partnership language

What bids are forcing?
What bids are encouraging?
What bids are discouraging?
Bids that suggest a willingness to quit are sometimes called "sign-offs."
The original bidder signs off in one of two ways:
1. By rebidding his own suit at the lowest possible level.
2. By rebidding 1 No Trump.
When the original bidder signs off, he does not imply that he wishes his partner to retire from the scene. He merely announces that his hand is in the minimum range; that is, 13 to 16 points. Responder must not abandon hope if it is still possible that the partnership has the equal of two opening bids (26 points). The opener, despite his sign-off, may have as many as 15 or 16 points.
Repeated bids in the same suit at minimum stages denote length of suit but no additional high-card values. For example:

♠ x   ♡ A Q 10 x x x   ◇ x x   ♣ A x x

OPENER	RESPONDER
1 ♡	1 ♠
2 ♡	2 NT
3 ♡	

The 3 Heart bid denotes a six-card suit but shows a hand with minimum high-card content. With more than that, opener would have contracted for game on the third round.

If opener had held:

♠ x ♡ A K J 10 x x ♢ x x ♣ A x x x

the bidding would have proceeded in the same way in the first two rounds, but after the 2 No Trump bid, opener would have gone on to 4 Hearts, not 3.

a mere preference by responder when he has not previously increased the contract is not encouraging

OPENER	RESPONDER
1 ♢	1 ♡
2 ♣	2 ♢

Responder has merely preferred Diamonds to Clubs, and his response did not increase the contract. He may have as little as 6 points.

He may have had:

♠ Q x x ♡ K J x x x ♢ 10 x x ♣ x x

but a preference shown by responder after he has
    previously increased the contract is en-
    couraging

OPENER	RESPONDER
1 ♡	2 ♣
2 ◇	2 ♡

The 2 Heart bid is constructive even though it is
made only as a preference. The reason is this: It be-
came clear that responder had some sort of Heart support. Why, then, did he take the trouble to bid 2 Clubs
instead of merely responding with a single raise to 2
Hearts? The answer is that his hand must have been
too good for a single raise. In other words, he had
more than 10 points. This might have been responder's hand:

♠ x x x   ♡ Q J x   ◇ x x   ♣ A K J x x

Similarly:

OPENER	RESPONDER
1 ♠	2 ◇
2 NT	3 ♠ ?

The 3 Spade bid is an aggressive call, not a mere
preference for Spades over No Trump. It is quite
apparent that responder has a good hand. He has
twice increased the contract. If he had a mediocre
hand he would have given an immediate raise to 2
Spades. He should have something like:

♠ K 10 x   ♡ x x x   ◇ A K J x x   ♣ x x

and is asking opener to choose between 4 Spades and
3 No Trump.

rebids by responder when opener makes a jump rebid (not forcing)

When opener jumps in the same suit (either his
own or partner's), responder need not bid again if his
response was below normal in strength.

OPENER	RESPONDER
1 ♠	1 NT
3 ♠	?

As responder you hold:

1. ♠ x x ♡ Q x x x ◇ 10 x x x ♣ K J x
2. ♠ x x ♡ K x x x ◇ K x x ♣ Q x x x

Holding No. 1, you should pass. You have the absolute minimum for a 1 No Trump response, 6 points.
Partner knows you have at least that much.

Holding No. 2, you should go on to 3 No Trump.
You have 8 points, which is in the upper bracket for
a No Trump response.

OPENER	RESPONDER
1 ♡	1 ♠
3 ♡	?

As responder you hold:

1. ♠ K J x x x x ♡ x x ◇ x x x ♣ x x
2. ♠ K J 10 x x ♡ J x x ◇ x x ♣ x x x

With No. 1 you should pass. You have less than a normal Spade response. Your hand is worth 6 points only at Spades, 4 in high cards and 2 for distribution.

With No. 2 you might choose to raise to 4 Hearts. While your response contained only 6 points, there are added factors, such as the three-card trump support and the doubleton Diamond. However, don't be surprised if partner goes down a trick at the 4 Heart contract.

As responder you hold:

♠ x x   ♡ K J x x x   ◇ x x x   ♣ J x x

The bidding has proceeded:

OPENER	RESPONDER
1 ◇	1 ♡
2 NT	?

Responder should pass. He has only 5 points for purposes of No Trump, which is below normal expectancy. It would be wrong to rebid Hearts. Partner would simply go on to game, which you should be persuaded is unattainable. Similarly, if opener's rebid has been 3 Hearts, responder should pass, because his response was worth only 6 points, even when valued at a Heart contract.

interpretation of various bids

The significance of the final bid is indicated in the following chart:

1.

OPENER	RESPONDER
1 ♠	3 ♠

Game force

2.

OPENER	RESPONDER
1 ♠	2 NT ?

Game force

3.

OPENER	RESPONDER
1 ♠	2 ♣ ?

One-round force

4.

OPENER	RESPONDER
Pass	1 ♠
3 ♠ ?	

Not forcing, strongly invitational

5.

OPENER	RESPONDER
Pass	1 ♠
2 ♡ ?	

Not forcing

6.

OPENER	RESPONDER
1 ♣	1 ◇
1 ♡ ?	

Not forcing

7.

OPENER	RESPONDER
1 ♡	1 ♠
3 ♠ ?	

Strongly invitational

8.

OPENER	RESPONDER
1 ♡	1 NT ?

Weak bid

9.

OPENER	RESPONDER
1 ♡	1 ♠
2 NT ?	

Strongly invitational

10.

OPENER	RESPONDER
1 ♠	2 ♠
3 ◇ ?	

One-round force

11.

OPENER	RESPONDER
1 ♡	1 ♠ ?
3 ♡	3 ♠ ?

Game force

12.

OPENER	RESPONDER
1 ♣	1 ♠
2 ♣ ?	

Not forcing

13.

OPENER	RESPONDER
1 ♠	2 ◇
2 ♠	3 ♣ ?

One-round force

14.

OPENER	RESPONDER
1 ♡	1 ♠
1 NT	2 ♣ ?

Not forcing

15.

OPENER	RESPONDER
1 NT	2 ♣ ?

Not forcing

16.

OPENER	RESPONDER
1 ♡	1 NT
2 ♠ ?	

Showing great strength

17.

OPENER	RESPONDER
1 ♡	2 ◇
3 ♣ ?	

Showing great strength

18.

OPENER	RESPONDER
1 ♠	2 ♠
2 NT	3 ♠ ?

Sign-off

19.

OPENER	RESPONDER
1 ◇	1 ♠
2 ♣	2 ◇ ?

Sign-off

20.

OPENER	RESPONDER
1 ♠	2 ♡
2 ♠ ?	

Not encouraging

21.

OPENER	RESPONDER
1 ♡	1 ♠
1 NT ?	

Not encouraging

22.

OPENER	RESPONDER
1 ♠	2 ♣
2 NT ?	

Strength showing

23.

OPENER	RESPONDER
1 ♠	2 ◇
2 ♠	3 ◇ ?

Mildly encouraging

24.

OPENER	RESPONDER
1 ♠	2 ◇
2 NT	3 ♠ ?

Game force

25.

OPENER	RESPONDER
1 ♡	1 ♠
4 ♡ ?	

Showing great strength

26.

OPENER	RESPONDER
1 ◇	1 ♠
4 ♠ ?	

Showing great strength

27.

OPENER	RESPONDER
1 ◇	1 ♡
1 NT	2 ♠ ?

Forcing

quiz no. 4: rebids by responders

(Answers follow this quiz)

1. You are South and hold:

   ♠ A Q J x x ♡ Q x x ◇ K Q x ♣ x x

   The bidding has proceeded:

NORTH	SOUTH
1 ♡	1 ♠
2 ♡	?

   What is your rebid?

2. You are South and hold:

   ♠ A Q J x x ♡ J x x ◇ Q J x ♣ x x

   The bidding has proceeded:

NORTH	SOUTH
1 ♡	1 ♠
2 ♡	?

   What is your rebid?

3. You are South and hold:

   ♠ xx   ♡ AKxxx   ◇ Jxx   ♣ Kxx

The bidding has proceeded:

NORTH	SOUTH
1 ♠	2 ♡
2 ♠	?

What is your rebid?

4. You are South and hold:

   ♠ 10xx   ♡ Kxx   ◇ AKJx   ♣ Qxx

The bidding has proceeded:

NORTH	SOUTH
1 ♣	1 ◇
1 NT	?

What is your rebid?

5. You are South and hold:

   ♠ 10xx   ♡ Kxx   ◇ AKxx   ♣ Jxx

The bidding has proceeded:

NORTH	SOUTH
1 ♣	1 ◇
1 NT	?

What is your rebid?

6. You are South and hold:

   ♠ xx   ♡ Qxxx   ◇ Axxx   ♣ Kxx

The bidding has proceeded:

NORTH	SOUTH
1 ♥	2 ♥
3 ♥	?

What is your rebid?

7. You are South and hold:

♠ Q x x   ♥ K x x   ◇ 10 x x x   ♣ A J x

The bidding has proceeded:

NORTH	SOUTH
1 ♥	2 ♥
3 ♥	?

What is your rebid?

8. You are South and hold:

♠ x x   ♥ Q x x x   ◇ K x x x   ♣ x x x

The bidding has proceeded:

NORTH	SOUTH
1 ♥	2 ♥
3 ♥	?

What is your rebid?

9. You are South and hold:

♠ A K J x x   ♥ Q x x   ◇ 10 x x   ♣ x x

The bidding has proceeded:

NORTH	SOUTH
1 ◇	1 ♠
2 ♠	?

What is your rebid?

10. You are South and hold:

♠ A Q 10 x x   ♡ K J x   ◇ J x x   ♣ x x

The bidding has proceeded:

NORTH	SOUTH
1 ◇	1 ♠
2 ♠	?

What is your rebid?

11. You are South and hold:

♠ J x x   ♡ 10 x   ◇ K J x x   ♣ K x x x

The bidding has proceeded:

NORTH	SOUTH
1 ♡	1 NT
2 NT	?

What is your rebid?

12. You are South and hold:

♠ J x x   ♡ x x x x   ◇ K Q 10 x x   ♣ x

The bidding has proceeded:

NORTH	SOUTH
1 ♣	1 ◇
1 ♠	?

What is your rebid?

13. You are South and hold:

♠ x   ♡ x x   ◇ A K Q x x x   ♣ x x x x

The bidding has proceeded:

NORTH	SOUTH
1 ♠	2 ♦
2 NT	?

What is your rebid?

14. You are South and hold:

♠ xx   ♡ 10xxx   ◇ KJx   ♣ Qxxx

The bidding has proceeded:

NORTH	SOUTH
1 ♠	1 NT
3 ♠	?

What is your rebid?

15. You are South and hold:

♠ xx   ♡ Kxx   ◇ Qxxx   ♣ Kxxx

The bidding has proceeded:

NORTH	SOUTH
1 ♠	1 NT
3 ♠	?

What is your rebid?

answers to quiz no. 4

1. Partner has announced by his opening bid that he has 13 points, which gives you a combined total of at least 26 points, and you have found a convenient place to play the hand; namely, in partner's rebid

suit. Do not bid 3 Hearts, inviting him to bid again, but bid 4 Hearts yourself.

2. Your hand has the value of 11 points, and partner has announced 13. You are not quite in a position to guarantee that a game contract should be assumed, nor are you willing to pass since the combined totals of your hand and partner's are known to be at least 24 points. Invite him to go to game, if he has a top minimum opening, by bidding 3 Hearts.

3. Your hand is very close to an opening bid, and since it is opposite an opening bid, you should be willing to try once more. The proper way to do so is to bid 2 No Trump. You have 11 points in high cards and partner might have 14.

4. Partner's opening bid guarantees 13 points, and since you have 13 and a hand that is suitable for No Trump play, you should go directly to game by bidding 3 No Trump.

5. Partner has shown at least 13 points by virtue of his opening bid and you have 11, which brings the combined total to 24. This is close enough to warrant your trying again. With your balanced distribution you should do so by bidding 2 No Trump, which invites partner to carry on if he has any values beyond the minimum.

6. Your hand is worth 10 points in support of a Heart bid, 9 in high cards and 1 for the doubleton. Your 2 Heart response shows a hand which contains 6 to 10 points, and partner is asking you to go to game with a hand that contains 8, 9, or 10 points, since you might have had only 6 or 7. Bid 4 Hearts.

7. Since you had the top limit for your 2 Heart raise—namely, 10 points—accept the invitation to go to game, but do so by bidding 3 No Trump. If partner passes, that should prove to be the best contract.

8. You have 6 points in support of a Heart bid, and partner is asking you if you have more values. Since you do not, there is no question that you have no choice but to pass.

9. Partner has opened the bidding and raised you, which shows that he has at least 14 points. You have 11 points yourself. Bid 3 Spades, which asks partner to contract for game if he has anything more.

10. When partner opens the bidding, then raises your suit, he guarantees at least 14 points. Since you have 12, you know the combined total is 26 and you should therefore contract for game yourself. Bid 4 Spades.

11. When you make a negative response of 1 No Trump and partner raises to 2 No Trump, he is asking you to go to 3 if your bid was made on 8 or 9 points, and to pass if the No Trump call contained only 6 or 7 points. Here you have 8 points and should accept his invitation. Bid 3 No Trump.

12. Since you responded with a bottom limit of 6 points, there is no necessity to speak again. The opening bidder's second bid of 1 Spade is not forcing, and the best way to describe your hand is by passing.

13. 3 No Trump. Partner's opening bid and subsequent rebid show a hand which contains 16 to 17 points. Your hand should produce 6 tricks in the play. Do not make the mistake of sounding discouraging by bidding 3 Diamonds. Go to game in No Trump with full confidence.

14. Partner's jump is begging you to continue if you have any reason to do so. However, when you respond 1 No Trump, holding 6 points, you announce all your values. Since you have no more, a pass is indicated.

15. Partner's jump is asking you to continue if you have any values in excess of those announced by your No Trump response. Since you hold 8 points when you might only have had 6, you should bid. In this case, with potential stoppers in the adverse suits, bid 3 No Trump and let partner make the final decision.

slam bidding

In slam bidding, the diagnosis is more important than the treatment. That is, the estimate that the partnership has 12 or 13 winners has much more importance than learning that you have all the Aces and Kings—only to discover that you can win only 10 or 11 tricks. Where No Trump bids are involved, the calculation is relatively simple. The total points in the pack are 40, and only high-card points are counted.

If your side has 33 points, a small slam may be available. It is not necessary in this case to check up on Aces because it is impossible for the opponents to have two Aces when you have 33 points. They can have, at most, only 7 points.

Similarly, when your side has 37 points, you may have a grand slam because it is impossible for the opponents to have an Ace. Remember, they can have at most only 3 points.

How do we determine that there are 33 or 34 points in the combined hands? Usually by simple addition. For example, you hold:

♠ K J x x x ♡ Q x ◇ A x x ♣ A x x

Partner opens with 1 Club; you respond 1 Spade; partner bids 3 Spades. You should sense a slam. How much is your hand worth? It had an original valuation of 15 points. Now that partner has supported Spades, you add 1 for the fifth Spade, giving your hand a true value of 16. Your partner, by opening and jumping, has shown that his hand is above the minimum range. (The minimum range is 13 to 16.) You may therefore count on him for at least 17 points; 17 plus 16 equals 33.

Let's look at it in another way. You have a good substantial opening bid yourself. With such a holding, if your partner opens and then jumps, you may expect to make a slam. In this particular case I suggest that you go right ahead and bid 6 Spades without asking any questions. When you have enough "stuff" for a slam, it is perfectly appropriate to bid it without engaging in elaborate ceremonies.

♠ A K x x ♡ J x x ◇ A J x ♣ Q x x

Partner opens with 1 Club; you respond 1 Spade; partner jumps to 2 No Trump. What do you bid?

You have 15 points; partner has 19 or 20. The combined total is 34 or 35—a cinch for a little slam and yet no chance of reaching 37 or 38. Bid 6 No Trump.

Let us assume the bidding has proceeded:

OPENER	RESPONDER
1 ♠	2 ◇
2 NT	?

Opener, by rebidding 2 No Trump, has shown a hand that is worth about 16 points. If your own hand totals 17 or more points in high cards, you should go all out to reach a slam.

diagnosis by opener

The opening bidder himself may become aware of slam possibilities as soon as he hears partner's response.

Whenever you open the bidding and partner makes a response that is forcing to game (such as 1 Spade to 3 Spades, or 1 Spade to 2 No Trump), you know that his hand is 13 to 15 points (the equal of an opening bid). If you have 13 to 15 points, there will be no slam, since the partnership assets will amount to 26 to 30 points.

But if you have 18 or 19, or more, there will be a slam.

If responder's reply has been in No Trump, you can tell within 2 points of what he has, and by simple addition can determine whether or not there is a chance for slam. For example:

♠ A Q 10 x x ♡ A 10 ◇ K J ♣ A x x x

You open with 1 Spade; partner responds 2 No Trump. You have 18 points; partner has between 13 and 15. If he has a maximum 2 No Trump of 15, you will have enough for a slam (33 will do with a five-card suit). If he has only 13, you will not have enough. You inquire by overbidding the game to 4 No Trump. *This is not a Blackwood bid. It is a raise of the No Trump bid and invites partner to bid a slam if he has a maximum 2 No Trump.*

♠ A x ♡ K Q 10 x x ◇ K J 9 ♣ A x x

You open with 1 Heart; partner responds 3 No Trump. You have 17 points; partner has at least 16; 33 with a five-card suit is sufficient. Bid 6 No Trump.

♠ A x x   ♡ x x x   ◇ K x x   ♣ A K x x

You open with 1 Club; partner responds 3 No Trump. You have 14 points and partner has between 16 and 18, so that even if he has a maximum 3 No Trump you will have only 32 points, which is insufficient for slam purposes. You therefore pass.

♠ A K 10 x x   ♡ x x   ◇ K Q x   ♣ A x x

You open with 1 Spade; partner responds 3 Spades. You have 16 points in high cards without counting the value of the fifth Spade or the doubleton. Partner is known to have between 13 and 16 points. If he has a minimum, slam will be improbable. If he has a near maximum, there will be a good chance for slam. Bid 4 Clubs and let partner take over. On this type of hand Blackwood is out, for a contract of 5 might not be safe. It will be noted that the distribution is not too favorable for slam purposes. If the doubleton Heart were a singleton, the prospects would be considerably brighter.

While for all general purposes a singleton in the opener's hand carries no weight at all, when a slam is in contemplation the singleton is a decided asset, for it affords secondary control of the suit; that is, it prevents the opponents from cashing two tricks in that suit and provides declarer with the chance to get to work with the development of the hand.

♠ A K 10 x x   ♡ x   ◇ K Q J x   ♣ A x x

You open with 1 Spade; partner jumps to 3 Spades. Here the slam is a virtual certainty, and a contract of 6 Spades is recommended. Just to make sure that partner has not made a jump without an Ace, you may check up with a Blackwood bid.

♠ A K 10 x x   ♡ x   ◇ K Q J x   ♣ A Q x

Here your hand is worth in excess of 20 points, and serious consideration should be given to a grand slam. You may bid 4 Clubs, showing the Ace, or you may embark on a Blackwood bid. Where responder makes a jump shift, the opener may diagnose a slam with very few excess values. Since the jump shift shows at least 19 points, 32 points in the combined hands are already assured.

a cue bid

When either partner makes a bid in the opponent's suit, it indicates the ability to win the first trick of that suit, either with the Ace or by trumping. This is a device used to suggest a slam and is forcing to game.

♠ none   ♡ K J x x x   ◇ K Q J x   ♣ A J 10 x

Partner opens with 1 Heart; opponent bids 1 Spade. You may bid 2 Spades. Naturally, such a bid should be made only with ample trump support and sufficient high-card values to justify your suspicion that there is a slam in the woodpile. Don't use this type of cue bid just to get to game.

slam diagnosis and development

♠ x   ♡ A Q 10 x x   ◇ K Q J   ♣ A x x x

You open with 1 Heart; partner raises to 3. Your hand had an original valuation of 18 points. When

partner supports Hearts, you add a point for the fifth
Heart, bringing it up to 19 points. Partner has at
least 13, so you are surely at the threshold of a slam.
You may bid 4 Clubs, showing the Ace (Hearts have
been agreed upon). If partner merely returns to 4
Hearts, you will know that he either has no Ace to
show or has such a minimum raise that he does not
choose to show it. If he chooses to go on from this
point, you will welcome his conversation. On this type
of hand you may check on partner's Aces by bidding
4 No Trump.

♠ K J 10 x   ♡ K Q J x   ◇ x x x   ♣ A x

Partner opens with 1 Club; you respond with 1
Spade; partner raises to 3. You have 15 points, facing
a partner who has opened and jumped. This suggests
a slam. Bid 4 Clubs. This shows the Ace rather than
Club support, for Spades have been agreed upon. If
partner bids 4 Diamonds, you should chance the slam
yourself. If partner bids 4 Hearts, showing the Ace
of that suit, you should either bid 5 Hearts, showing
the King, or jump to 5 Spades, asking partner to bid
the slam if he has not two losing Diamonds.

♠ J x   ♡ J x x   ◇ A K x x x   ♣ K J x

Partner opens with 1 Heart; you respond 2 Diamonds; partner bids 3 Hearts. You have 13 points in
high cards opposite a partner who has opened and
jumped. A slam is therefore probable. Normally, we
suggest this by showing an Ace, but since you have
none to show, you must suggest slam by overbidding
the game with 5 Hearts. To bid merely 4 Hearts
would be grossly inadequate and would show no

special strength beyond the mere 11 which you, by your 2 Diamond bid, suggested.

♠ J x   ♡ A K x x x x   ♢ A x x   ♣ x x

Partner opens with 1 Spade; you respond 2 Hearts; partner raises to 3 Hearts. This looks like a slam. Partner has a little bit more than an opening bid, and you have more than an opening bid. Bid 4 Diamonds, showing the Ace. If partner returns to 4 Hearts, try once more by bidding 5 Hearts. If partner, over 4 Diamonds, shows the Ace of Clubs, bid 6 Hearts.

the blackwood convention

Don't become a victim of the propaganda that the Blackwood convention is easy to learn. On the contrary, it requires a great deal of practice and experience. True enough, it is easy to learn the responses set forth below, but it is not easy to learn when to use it and when not to use it. At a reasonable estimate you should use it on about one slam hand out of four. The other three should be bid in what I call the direct method, either by the up-and-at-them method or by each partner's showing his own Aces individually and voluntarily. Use Blackwood when the *only* thing you are concerned with is Aces.

When the preliminary rounds of bidding have indicated that a slam is probable and a suit has been agreed upon, either player may institute the convention by calling 4 No Trump. No special holding is required, but the player making the 4 No Trump bid must be quite convinced that the hand will play safely for eleven tricks.

The responses are:

With no Aces, bid 5 Clubs.
With one Ace, bid 5 Diamonds.

With two Aces, bid 5 Hearts.
With three Aces, bid 5 Spades.
With four Aces, bid 5 No Trump.

After Aces have been shown, the 4 No Trump bidder may ask for Kings by bidding 5 No Trump. However, there is the very distinct proviso that the *5 No Trump bid must never be made unless it has been previously determined that the partnership is in possession of all 4 Aces.*

In other words, the opener, late in the bidding, calls 4 No Trump. Responder bids 5 Diamonds, showing one Ace. The opener now bids 5 No Trump, asking for Kings. Responder knows that the opener has three Aces. Otherwise he could not tell that the partnership has all four Aces and would not be privileged to call for Kings.

The responder to the 5 No Trump bid shows the number of his Kings exactly as he shows the number of his Aces in response to the 4 No Trump bid.

Where the agreed suit is Clubs, the 4 No Trump bidder must, in that case, have at least two Aces, because otherwise the partnership will be in a slam after a 5 Diamond response, and the opposition will hold two Aces.

It is essential to determine whether or not information concerning how many Aces partner has will solve your problem. After all, many a hand with all the Aces has no chance to produce a slam. A singleton or even a doubleton in partner's hand may be the decisive factor.

As a general rule, the stronger of the two hands should be given the opportunity to start the convention, because he can better judge what the hands will produce. For example:

♠ xxx ♡ Axxx ♢ Kxx ♣ Axx

You should not employ the Blackwood convention yourself, for the information about how many Aces and Kings your partner has will not solve your problem of the trick-taking capacity of the hand. With holdings of this type, you should offer partner the opportunity to employ Blackwood. When you advise him that you have two Aces and the King, he will be in a much superior position to determine the possibilities of the hand.

Holding:

♠ x   ♡ K Q J x x x   ♢ A K   ♣ K Q 10 x

♠ A Q x   ♡ A K J x x x   ♢ A x   ♣ K Q

you are in a splendid position to employ Blackwood, for your only concern is the matter of Aces and Kings.

It is a provision of the Blackwood convention that the 4 No Trump bidder is the captain of the team. When he ascertains the Aces and Kings held by partner, he, and only he, has the prerogative of deciding on the final contract. The responder has no further voice in the proceedings.

It must be pointed out that a void in the responding hand is not treated as equivalent to an Ace in responding to a 4 No Trump bid. While on the subject of voids, it may be well to observe that a player who holds a void suit is not in strategic position to make a Blackwood bid. If he finds out that his partner has an Ace, he will not know whether the Ace happens to be in that suit. With the following hand:

♠ A K Q x x   ♡ K Q J x   ♢ A Q J x   ♣ none

when partner supports Spades, it would be pointless to employ Blackwood. If you find out he has 1 Ace, the knowledge will not be helpful to you. Instead of

asking for Aces, you tell about them; you show the
Ace of Diamonds and hope that partner will show
the Ace of Hearts.

when a 4 no trump bid is not Blackwood

*When your side has not mentioned a suit, the 4
No Trump bid is not Blackwood.* Therefore, an opening bid of 4 No Trump indicates a hand that is somewhat stronger than an opening 3 No Trump bid and
denotes the possession of 28, 29, or 30 points.

Where the opponent opens a pre-emptive bid of
4 Spades and your partner bids 4 No Trump, that is
not Blackwood. Since no suit has been mentioned, obviously the 4 No Trump bid cannot be conventional;
4 No Trump in this case forces partner to name his
best suit.

In all cases where responder has raised an opening
bid of 1, 2, or 3 No Trump to 4 No Trump, again no
suit has been mentioned. Obviously, the 4 No Trump
bid cannot be conventional. It merely asks partner
to continue toward slam if his opening was maximum,
and to pass if his opening was minimum.

*A 4 No Trump bid is not Blackwood when you are
raising a No Trump bid which your partner has previously made.* But a sudden burst to 4 No Trump when
a suit has apparently been agreed upon is a Blackwood bid. For example:

SOUTH	WEST	NORTH	EAST
1 ♠	4 ♡	4 ♠	Pass
4 NT			

Since it is apparent that Spades are agreed upon,
South's 4 No Trump bid is Blackwood. It seems highly

unlikely that South would prefer No Trump to Spades in the above sequence. Similarly:

OPENER	RESPONDER
1 ♠	3 ♠
4 NT	

Where a previous slam signal has been given, a 4 No Trump bid is to be construed as Blackwood.

defensive bidding

overcalls

"Overcall" is a term used to describe a bid made by you after the opponents have opened the bidding, but before your partner has entered the auction.

In making overcalls, too much reliance should not be placed on point count. The consideration of paramount importance is the texture of your trump suit. *When you overcall at the level of 2, you should promise partner that you won't lose more than two tricks in the trump suit itself.* Beware of overcalling with suits like this, especially at the level of 2:

> A Q x x x
> K J x x x
> Q 10 x x x

Where your bid will serve as a good lead director to partner, you should lean in favor of overcalls. For example:

> ♠ A K J x x ♡ x x x ◇ x x ♣ x x x

> ♠ K Q J x x ♡ K x x ◇ x x ♣ x x x

The opening bid has been 1 Club. Overcall with 1 Spade. This is a good lead-directing bid and may prevent the opponent from romping off with a 3 No Trump contract.

Overcalls in suits in which you cannot stand the lead are frowned upon by this department.

♠ x x   ♡ A x x   ◇ J x x x x   ♣ A x x

If opponent opens with 1 Club, I am against overcalling 1 Heart.

the jump overcall

One way of showing strength when an adversary opens the bidding is by a jump overcall; that is, a bid of exactly one more than necessary to overcall. This jump is not a force but a strong invitation, which partner is expected to accept if he has anything at all.

The jump overcall is made on a hand that contains either two good long suits or a long and strong suit with values concentrated mostly in that suit and some side strength. For example:

♠ x   ♡ x x   ◇ A K J x   ♣ A Q J 10 x x

Opponent bids 1 Spade. Make a jump overcall of 3 Clubs.

♠ x x   ♡ A K Q x x x x   ◇ x   ♣ A Q J

Opponent opens 1 Diamond. Make a jump overcall of 2 Hearts.

the 1 no trump overcall

To overcall an adverse opening bid of 1 No Trump,
a player should have the equal of a normal opening
1 No Trump bid (16 to 19 points), and the adverse
suit must be safely stopped.

take-out double

When an opponent opens the bidding and you have
the equal of an opening bid or more, the most usual
way to indicate such strength is by a take-out double.

It is important to differentiate between a take-out
double and one that is intended for penalties. A
double is intended for take-out:

1. When partner has made no bid or double.
2. When the double is of 1, 2, or 3 of a suit.
3. When the double is made at the doubler's first
opportunity to double that suit.

All three ingredients must be present.

A double of 2 No Trump is always for penalties.

A double of 1 No Trump is primarily for penalties,
but partner may refuse to leave it in if his hand lacks
defensive strength. Note the following example:

SOUTH	WEST	NORTH	EAST
1 ♠	Pass	1 NT	Pass
2 ♣	Double		

This is not a take-out double, as it was not made at
the first opportunity to double Spades.

♠ K J x x   ♡ x   ◇ A Q x x   ♣ A x x x

EAST	SOUTH
1 ♡	Double

This is a take-out double. You have an opening bid but wish partner to name his best suit. You will then have found the best vehicle if your side is to play the contract. A take-out double may be repeated when the opponents have interfered and prevented partner from bidding. For example, as South you hold:

♠ K J x x   ♡ A J x x   ◇ x   ♣ A K x x

EAST	SOUTH	WEST	NORTH
1 ◇	Double	2 ◇	Pass
Pass	?		

Repeat your take-out double, insisting on a bid from partner, though he is known to have a weak hand.

With the same holding, if the bidding has proceeded:

SOUTH	WEST	NORTH	EAST
1 ♣	1 ◇	Pass	Pass
?			

you should double, affording partner the opportunity to bid 1 Spade, 1 Heart, or return to 2 Clubs. Note that a player who has previously opened the bidding may make a take-out double if partner has not yet bid. Both these actions indicate holdings above the minimum required for opening the bidding.

requirements for a take-out double

Normally, a take-out double announces about 13 points and the ability to support any suit partner might bid, or a good suit of your own to fall back on in case of fire.

Be prepared for partner's response in your weakest suit. If you are unable to cope with such a response, the double is unsound, even if your hand contains more than 13 points. For example:

♠ K 10 x x   ♡ x   ◇ K Q x x   ♣ A x x x

If your right-hand opponent opens with 1 Spade, it would be unsound to double. Partner will almost surely bid 2 Hearts, leaving you no safe parking place.

double of 1 no trump

The double of 1 No Trump is primarily for penalties, but partner of the doubler may exercise his own judgment.

An immediate double of an opening 1 No Trump bid should be made only on a hand that is at least as good as the opening bidder's; that is, at least 16 points. Therefore, when partner of the doubler has at least 6 points, he should leave the double in. Sixteen plus 6 equals 22, which means the opposition can have no more than 18, and you should therefore be able to outscore them.

responses to take-out doubles

The following table is recommended to assist you in forming an estimate of your holding when responding to a take-out double:

A hand containing 6 points is a fair hand.

A hand containing 9 points is a good hand.

A hand containing 11 points is a probable game hand.

In using this table, count high-card and distributional points.

Partner doubles 1 Heart. You hold:

(A)	(B)
♠ K Q 10 x x	♠ K Q 10 x x
♡ x x x	♡ x x x
◇ x x x	◇ x x
♣ x x	♣ K x x
(c)	(D)
♠ K Q 10 x x	♠ K Q 10 x x x
♡ x x x	♡ x x x
◇ x x	◇ x
♣ K Q x	♣ K J x

(A) contains 6 points and is a fair hand. (B) contains 9 points and is a good hand. (c) and (D) contain 11 points each and therefore are probable game hands. You should respond with one more than is necessary—that is, 2 Spades—on the last two.

The requirement for responding to partner's take-out double is zero points. The less you have, the more urgent it is to respond, else opponents will make their doubled contract with overtricks which can prove very costly. Do not pass because you are in distress. In responding to partner's take-out double, prefer a four-card major to a five-card minor at the level of 1. For example:

    ♠ A x x x ♡ x x ◇ x x ♣ Q 10 x x x

Partner doubles 1 Heart. Respond 1 Spade rather than 2 Clubs.

Your partner doubles 1 Diamond. You hold:

    ♠ A J x x ♡ K J x x ◇ x x ♣ x x x

Your hand has the value of 10 points. It is therefore a good hand. You should arrange to bid both suits in their logical order, showing Spades first.

In responding to a take-out double, prefer a major suit to 1 No Trump, but prefer 1 No Trump to a minor suit if you hold a fairly good hand; that is, about 9 points in high cards. For example, partner doubles a bid of 1 Heart and you hold:

    ♠ A 9 x ♡ Q J 9 x ◇ x x ♣ Q 10 x x

Your best response is 1 No Trump. This hand contains 9 points and has a double Heart stopper. This is preferable to responding 2 Clubs.

Your partner doubles 1 Heart and you hold:

    ♠ K 9 x x ♡ K J x ◇ x x x ♣ Q x x

While the hand has the strength to justify a 1 No Trump response to partner's double (9 points), a bid of 1 Spade is to be preferred.

responding with strong hands

When you hold a hand with 11 or more points (or a little bit less with a long suit), you should so advise partner by bidding one more than necessary in response, even though your suit is not very impressive.

♠ A Q x ♡ K x x x ◊ K x x ♣ x x x

Partner has doubled 1 Club. Your proper response is 2 Hearts, despite the weakness of the suit.

♠ Q J 10 ♡ Q x x ◊ K J x ♣ K x x x

Partner has doubled 1 Diamond. Respond 2 No Trump. Such a bid should rarely be made with a point count of less than 12.

♠ x x ♡ A x x ◊ Q J 9 ♣ K Q J 10 x

Partner has doubled 1 Spade. Respond 3 Clubs.

procedure by doubler's partner after an intervening bid

When partner has doubled the opening bid and your right-hand opponent inserts a bid, you are relieved of your obligation to speak. But if you hold 8 points, counting both high cards and distribution, you should have the desire to bid. For example:

♠ K 10 x x x ♡ J x x ◊ K x x ♣ x x

♠ Q 10 x x x ♡ x x x ◊ K Q x ♣ x x

The bidding has proceeded:

WEST	NORTH	EAST	SOUTH
1 ♣	Double	1 ♡	?

With both of these hands you should make a free bid of 1 Spade. You have 8 points—7 in high cards and 1 for distribution—so you have a fairly good hand, which justifies a free bid at the level of 1.

action by doubler

The doubler should exercise caution in offering raises to a partner whom he has forced to bid.

As South you hold:

♠ KQxx ♡ Qxxx ◊ x ♣ AQxx

The bidding has proceeded:

EAST	SOUTH	WEST	NORTH
1 ◊	Double	Pass	1 ♠
Pass	?		

You should raise only to 2 Spades. Remember, partner may have no values.

The above hand was valued at 15 points when you doubled—13 in high cards and 2 for distribution. However, since partner has responded in the suit which you can support, you may revalue your hand as dummy. The singleton, therefore, becomes worth 3 points in the dummy hand, and your hand now has the value of 16 points.

When contemplating a raise of partner's suit, the

following is a reasonably accurate guide for a take-out doubler:

With 16 points, you may go to the 2 level.
With 19 points, you may go to the 3 level.
With 22 points, you may go to the 4 level.

action by doubler's partner when doubler raises

When your partner doubles and then raises you, you should feel impelled to bid again with any inducement. For example:

1. ♠ K x x   ♡ J 10 x x   ◇ x x   ♣ A x x x

2. ♠ A x x   ♡ J 10 x x   ◇ x x   ♣ A x x x

Partner has doubled a bid of 1 Diamond, you respond 1 Heart, and partner raises to 2 Hearts. With No. 1, you should bid 3 Hearts. You have a good hand (9 points, 8 in high cards and 1 for the doubleton). With No. 2, you should go to game. Your hand has the value of 10 points, 9 in high cards and 1 for the doubleton; and partner, by his double and raise, has shown that his hand has the value of at least 16 points, which brings the known combined total to the necessary 26. Do not be concerned about the texture of your trump suit. Partner must have allowed for it. Always remember this: As far as your partner is concerned, you might have had nothing.

action by opener's partner over a double

1. With a strong hand, redouble. (A holding of 11 or more points, even without trump support for partner, justifies a redouble.)

2. With a bad hand, pass (less than 6 points).

3. With in-between hands containing 6 to 9 points, it is better to bid immediately.

Partner opens with 1 Spade, second hand doubles, and you hold:

1. ♠ x   ♡ K J x x   ◊ K Q x x   ♣ A x x x

2. ♠ x x   ♡ K x x x   ◊ A K J x x   ♣ x x

3. ♠ Q x x x   ♡ x   ◊ x x x x   ♣ Q x x x

4. ♠ x x   ♡ x x x   ◊ A K J x x   ♣ x x x

With Nos. 1 and 2, redouble, even though you lack support for partner. Your hand is more than 11 points in high cards. Partner must pass the opponent's take-out around to you, which you intend to double for penalties.

With No. 3, raise to 2 Spades. It is a weak hand, but your bid serves the purpose of making things a little more difficult for doubler's partner.

With No. 4, bid 2 Diamonds. This hand is neither good nor bad, but this is the only time it will be convenient for you to show your suit.

overcall in opponent's suit

(THE IMMEDIATE CUE BID)

This is the most powerful of defensive calls and is the equivalent of an opening 2 demand bid. It is forcing to game. It announces the ability to win the first trick in the adverse suit. For example, an opponent opens with 1 Diamond. You hold:

♠ K Q 10 x   ♡ A Q J x x   ◊ void   ♣ A Q J x

You wish to insist upon a game even if partner has no strength. The proper bid is 2 Diamonds, forcing to game.

the 3 no trump overcall

This bid evidences the desire to play at that contract. Partner should not rescue with any five- or six-card suit unless game can be made in that suit.

This bid is usually made with a long minor suit that can be run. For example, the opening bid is 3 Hearts. You hold:

♠ x x   ♡ K x   ◇ A x   ♣ A K Q 10 x x x

Overcall with 3 No Trump.

penalty doubles

A double is for penalties (as distinguished from a take-out double):

1. When the doubler's partner has previously indicated strength, as by bidding or doubling.

2. Whenever the double is of 4 or more of a suit.

3. Whenever the doubler has had a previous opportunity to make a take-out double of that suit but has failed to do so.

4. Whenever the double is of a No Trump contract. Doubles of 1 No Trump are primarily for penalty, but partner may exercise the option to take them out with little or no defensive strength.

Point count is not a complete guide for purposes of making penalty doubles in suit bids. But in making penalty doubles in No Trump contracts, it may be applied with accuracy.

Penalty doubles should be made on a strictly businesslike basis. Count those tricks which you expect to win, add them to the number that partner is expected to win, and let that be your guide.

When partner opens the bidding and your opponent overcalls in the suit which you had the desire to bid, double for penalties. For example:

♠ K J 9 x   ♡ Q x x x   ◇ A x x x   ♣ x

Partner opens with 1 Club; opponent overcalls with 1 Spade. Since your bid would have been 1 Spade had your opponent passed, you should double for penalties.

When partner opens and opponent overcalls and you are tempted to bid 2 No Trump, you will obtain better results by doubling instead. For example:

NORTH	EAST	SOUTH
1 ♠	2 ♡	?

♠ x x   ♡ K J 9 x   ◇ A x x x   ♣ Q x x

Do not bid 2 No Trump. Double.

As a safety factor, do not double for penalty unless you expect to beat the contract by at least two tricks. You may, however, double a bid of 2 Clubs or 2 Diamonds with a little bit less, since the contract, if fulfilled, will not produce a game.

For purposes of business doubles, count your probable tricks in the following manner:

Where partner opens with 1 of a suit, count on him for three tricks.

Where partner opens with 1 No Trump, count on him for four tricks.

Where partner has made a take-out double, count on him for three tricks.

Where partner has overcalled or has given you a single raise, count on him for only one trick.

Where partner has made a pre-emptive bid, count on him for no tricks.

Against a suit contract, do not count on more than two tricks in one suit. Where your suit is long and partner has supported it, do not expect to win more than one trick in that suit.

Be slow to double when you have length in partner's suit. Be quick to double when short in partner's suit.

Count one defensive trick for a holding of four adverse trumps, even though they are small ones.

opening leads

table of opening leads

HOLDING IN SUIT	AGAINST NO TRUMP BIDS	AGAINST TRUMP BIDS
A K Q J	A	K
A K Q x x x	A	K
A K Q x x	K	K
A K Q x	K	K
A K x	K	K
A K J 10 x	J	K
A K J 10	A	K
A K J x	A	K
A K 10 x	K	K
A K J x x	x	K
A K J x x x x	A	K
A K x x x x	x	K
A K 10 9 x	10	K
A K 10 9 x x	10	K
A K x x x	x	K
A Q J x x	Q	A
K Q J x x	K	K

HOLDING IN SUIT	AGAINST NO TRUMP BIDS	AGAINST TRUMP BIDS
K Q 10 x x	K	K
K Q 7 4 2	4	K
Q J 10 x x	Q	Q
Q J 9 x x	Q	Q
Q J 7 4 2	4	4
J 10 9 x x	J	J
J 10 8 x x	J	J
J 10 7 4 2	4	4
10 9 8	10	10
10 9 7 4	4	10
A Q 10 9 x	10[1]	A
A Q 8 7 4 2	7	A
A J 10 8 2	J	A
A 10 9 7 2	10	A
K J 10 7 2	J	J
K 10 9 7 2	10	10
Q 10 9 7 2	10	10
A J 4	4	4
A 7 4	4	A
K J 4	4[2]	4
K 7 4	4	4
Q 10 4	4	4
J 7 4	4	4
K 9 8 7	7[3]	7

[1] The Queen is led when you suspect the King is in dummy.
[2] Unattractive lead, but made necessary by the bidding.
[3] Do not treat the 9-8-7 as the top of an inferior sequence because partner may improperly read it as the top of nothing.

opening leads

It has been said that any good pair granted the imaginary privilege of being able to make the double dummy lead on every hand would be virtually assured of winning any national championship in which they participated. If this is true, the importance of the opening lead immediately becomes apparent.

The term "lead" refers to the first card played at each trick, whether by defense or declarer. In this chapter, however, we shall be concerned only with the defensive lead to the first trick. In other words, the opening lead.

There are a number of bromides current advocating such ideas as "Never lead away from a King," or "Never lead away from an Ace," "Always lead the highest of your partner's suit," etc. Some of these have a sound basis. Others have none. However, this general truth should be borne in mind by the reader: that the selection of the opening lead is not an exact science. There is great room for the exercise of the imagination, and on a given hand a number of experts might disagree in the choice of an opening lead.

In selecting opening leads, it is advisable to get into the habit of classifying various hands. A lead may be proper against a No Trump contract which, with the same hand, would be improper against a suit contract. You must ask yourself, "Am I leading against a part score, a game, or a slam contract? Has my partner bid? Has my partner suggested a lead to me? Will the opponents probably make this hand or will they go down?"

leads at no trump

We shall take up those hands where no specific information has been obtained from the bidding. For example:

NORTH	SOUTH
1 NT	2 NT
3 NT	

Against No Trump contracts it is essential to develop tricks out of small cards.

Against a suit contract, if you hold A-K-7-4-3, you would hardly expect to take more than the Ace and the King. But at No Trump there is a very good chance that you will take tricks with the small cards. Therefore, your longest suit should usually be selected as the opening lead.

One of the outstanding weaknesses of the ordinary player is a tendency to lead new suits each time he obtains the lead. It has been estimated that every time the defense leads a new suit it averages to lose a half trick, so that it is generally a good policy to stick to the suit you open unless you have a good reason for shifting.

The most desirable lead is from the top of a complete sequence.

♠ 9 6 4
♡ 7 3
◇ J 10 9 6
♣ K J 5 2

In this hand the Jack of Diamonds is a much more desirable lead than the 2 of Clubs because it is certain

not to lose a trick regardless of the adverse holding;
whereas the Club lead might permit declarer to win
a trick with the Queen, which he might not otherwise
have been able to do.

♠ Q 6 3 2
♡ 9 6 3
◇ 8 2
♣ Q 10 8 3

I would recommend a Club lead rather than a
Spade because the Club holding is more nearly a
sequence. Notice that if your partner holds only the
Jack of Clubs you have not lost a trick. In fact, you
are well on your way to develop two tricks in that
suit. If, however, you lead a Spade and again find
your partner with the Jack, you are still not certain
to build up a trick unless your partner also has the 10.

Where you have a choice between two suits of exactly the same texture, it is the general practice to
lead the major suit rather than the minor, the theory
being that the opponents will sometimes conceal a
minor suit but are less likely to conceal a major suit.

♠ Q 9 6 5
♡ 10 9 8 5
◇ 7 3
♣ 8 5 3

If I were forced to choose my opening lead between
the Spade and the Heart, I would select the Heart
because it is less likely to cost a trick. Quality should
take precedence over quantity. For example:

♠ Q J 10 9
♡ 8 3
◇ Q 7 4 3 2
♣ 6 3

The Queen of Spades is the proper lead. The Spade lead cannot lose a trick, whereas the Diamond lead may permit declarer to win with the Jack, which he might not otherwise have been able to do.

The lead from A-Q-6-2 is undesirable, but the lead from A-Q-6-4-2 is extremely desirable. In the first case, you are almost sure to give up a trick to declarer. In the second case, you are giving up the same trick, but when partner gets in and returns the suit, you have a reasonable expectancy of winning the four remaining tricks. The following hand illustrates the principle:

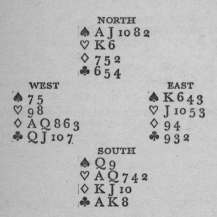

```
                    NORTH
                 ♠ A J 10 8 2
                 ♡ K 6
                 ◇ 7 5 2
                 ♣ 6 5 4
   WEST                          EAST
 ♠ 7 5                         ♠ K 6 4 3
 ♡ 9 8                         ♡ J 10 5 3
 ◇ A Q 8 6 3                   ◇ 9 4
 ♣ Q J 10 7                    ♣ 9 3 2
                    SOUTH
                 ♠ Q 9
                 ♡ A Q 7 4 2
                 ◇ K J 10
                 ♣ A K 8
```

If West should open the Queen of Clubs, declarer will win and take the Spade finesse, which loses to East. Now a Diamond shift comes too late, and the defense can take only two Diamonds and the King of Spades. But if the 6 of Diamonds is opened, declarer is forced to win with the Jack. Now when he takes the Spade finesse and East gets in, a Diamond return defeats the contract.

Where you have several high cards for entries, your longest suit invariably should be selected. For example:

♠ A 8 4 3
♡ 7 5
◊ Q 7 6 4 2
♣ A 5

The proper lead is the 4 of Diamonds, because even though you lose a trick at the opening, you hope to build up several tricks in that suit while you still have two Aces as entry cards.

♠ Q 8
♡ K J 5 3
◊ 10 4
♣ J 8 5 3 2

You have a choice between a weak five-card minor and a strong four-card major. The choice should be in favor of the Club, because there is a chance to develop more tricks with this suit if the suit breaks well for your side.

LEADING FROM BAD HANDS

It is sound policy not to waste efforts on a hopeless hand. For example:

♠ 10 9 4
♡ 10 8 5 4 2
◊ 7 3
♣ 5 3 2

Your hand, to all intents and purposes, is dead. It is poor policy to lead the fourth best Heart. Your

side's only trick-taking possibilities are in your partner's hand. The only thing you can do, therefore, is
to give him a fairly decent start in the race to take
tricks. Your best bet is the 10 of Spades, hoping
(somewhat against hope) that you may strike your
partner's best suit.

THE SHORT-SUIT LEAD

We have just observed the use of the short-suit lead
on hopeless hands. That type of lead is also made on
hands where you fear to lead anything else because
you have great hopes of taking tricks. For example:

♠ K 10 8
♡ J 4 3 2
◇ A Q 10 4
♣ 10 9

This presents no desirable opening lead. I regard
the Diamond as the most undesirable. If you adopt
waiting tactics, the declarer will probably never be
able to win a trick in that suit. If you lead the Diamond, he will almost surely take at least one trick.
The next in order of undesirability is the Spade. In
the first place, your partner will probably misread the
lead of the 8; second, you may very easily sacrifice a
trick by that lead. The Heart lead, therefore, appears
to be the logical one. However, experience has shown
that a lead from the Jack and three small cards is, in
the long run, not very profitable. From holdings such
as those in Spades, Hearts, and Diamonds, the best
results are obtained by waiting. By the process of
elimination, therefore, we arrive at the Club lead, and
the 10 of Clubs should be selected.

THE CARD TO LEAD WHEN YOUR PARTNER HAS BID AGAINST NO TRUMP DECLARATIONS

Where you have any two cards or three worthless cards of his suit, you lead the highest. Similarly, where you have two honors in sequence. In all other cases, the proper lead is a low card. The italicized card is the proper one to lead from partner's suit in the table which follows:

A*2*	K*2*	Q*2*	*9*2	*9*62	*7*54
A*6*2	K*6*2	Q*6*2	J*6*2	*10*62	A*6*32
K*6*32	Q*6*32	J*6*32	*9*632	*5*432	*9*6432
Q*J*62	K*Q*62	J*10*62			

Observe the following very usual holding:

NORTH
♠ 6 5

WEST
♠ Q 7 2

EAST
♠ A 10 9 8 4

SOUTH
♠ K J 3

East has bid Spades and South No Trump, expecting to take two Spade tricks. If West leads the Queen, South will win two tricks. The lead of the 2 of Spades enables the defense to capture South's Jack.

WHETHER TO LEAD PARTNER'S SUIT OR YOUR OWN

When in doubt whether to lead partner's suit or your own, give him the benefit of the doubt. Greater consideration should be given to a suit in which partner has overcalled than to one in which he has opened the bidding. He will open frequently on weak suits, but his overcall should be based on good suits. Holding a singleton is usually a good excuse, provided you have some hope of establishing tricks in your own hand. Even a singleton of partner's suit should be led if your hand is entirely hopeless.

Holding two small cards of your partner's suit, you have a slight excuse for not leading the suit. However, any five-card suit does not constitute that slight excuse. For example:

♠ 6 2
♡ 9 7 3
◇ J 8 6 4 2
♣ 7 5 2

Partner has bid Spades. The Diamond lead is not to be considered. Lead the 6 of Spades.

LEADING THE OPPONENT'S SUIT

Where your best suit contains a complete sequence, it should be led even though the opponents have bid it. For example:

♠ Q J 10 9 4
♡ Q 10 7 3
◇ 8 4
♣ 4 3

You should lead the Queen of Spades even though that suit has been bid by your right-hand opponent. If, however, your holding is:

♠ K J 8 3 2
♡ Q J 9 3
◇ 6 4
♣ 7 5

you have an entirely different situation. The lead of a
Spade will probably be into declarer's A-Q, thus
presenting him with a trick. In this case, the Queen
of Hearts is the proper lead.

Modern bidders very frequently open the bidding
with a Club when they do not really have that suit.
Therefore, when a Club lead is normal from your
hand, as a general rule you should not refrain from
leading it simply because the suit has been bid by
your right-hand opponent. For example:

♠ K 9 2
♡ 8 6
◇ A 4 3
♣ K J 9 4 3

If the bidding is opened on my right with a Club
and declarer subsequently plays No Trump, I would
open the 4 of Clubs. If partner has the Queen of the
suit, it will be established at once. If he has the 10,
there is a good chance to build up the suit while I
still have two likely entries.

LEADS AGAINST NO TRUMP WHEN PART-
NER HAS DOUBLED THE FINAL CONTRACT

A double of a No Trump contract made by a player
who does not have the opening lead carries certain
inferences regarding that opening lead.

1. If the doubler has bid a suit, the leader must
absolutely lead that suit even if he has only a
singleton and has a good suit of his own. For example:

♠ 7
♡ K Q J 8 5
◇ 7 3 2
♣ 8 6 4 3

Your partner has bid Spades and subsequently doubled 3 No Trump. You must lead the 7 of Spades, not the King of Hearts. Your partner has stated that if you lead Spades he will defeat the contract.

2. If the opening leader has bid a suit, partner's double requests him to lead that suit. For example:

♠ K J 8 6 3
♡ K Q J 3
◇ A 5
♣ 6 5

You have bid Spades. Partner has not participated in the auction until he doubled the opponents in the final 3 No Trump contract. Without the double your best lead would be the king of Hearts, but your partner's double is based on the belief that you will lead Spades, and you must not disappoint him.

3. If both partners have bid, it is not easy to determine which suit to lead when partner doubles. Use your own judgment.

4. When neither the leader nor the doubler has bid, the doubler is suggesting to partner to lead the dummy's first-bid suit unless the leader has a very good opening of his own. But bear in mind that this is only a suggestion—not a command.

Presume the bidding to have progressed as follows:

SOUTH	WEST	NORTH	EAST
1 ♡	Pass	1 ♠	Pass
2 NT	Pass	3 NT	Double
Pass			

You are West, holding the following hand:

♠ 9 2
♡ J 10 4 3
◇ 10 7 5 4
♣ K 8 4

Hearts have been bid by the declarer. Do not select that suit. It would not be good policy to lead the fourth best Diamond, hoping to establish that suit. Inasmuch as your partner doubled and you have no indicated lead, the 9 of Spades should be selected.

leads against suit contracts

Under this heading perhaps the soundest procedure is first to put the quietus on the popular superstition, "Never lead away from a King." It is no more risky to lead away from the King than it is from the Jack; in fact, I think it is much less risky. It is, however, a disadvantage to lead from any honor that is not any part of a sequence. There is this distinction between No Trump and suit play. At suit play, the lead away from an Ace is unorthodox and should be avoided. If that suit must be led on the opening lead, the proper lead is the Ace itself.

WHEN LEADING PARTNER'S SUIT

The same principles are applied against No Trump contracts. In other words, the highest of partner's suit is led only when you hold two cards, or three worthless cards in his suit, or a sequence. Of course the Ace is always led.

DESIRABLE SINGLETON LEADS

A singleton should not be led simply as a matter of course. The ideal conditions for the lead of a singleton are as follows:

1. Where you have control of trumps.

2. Where you have surplus trumps, holding A-x, A-x-x, or K-x-x.

3. Where partner has bid. This gives you a good chance to reach his hand in order to obtain the ruff.

4. Wherever the defense of the hand seems otherwise hopeless against slam contracts.

UNDESIRABLE SINGLETON LEADS

1. Where you hold K-x, Q-x-x, or Q-J-x of trump. In this case you are not at all sure that you wish to trump with this holding.

2. Whenever you hold four or more trumps, the singleton lead is usually undesirable. Your longest side suit should be led in an effort to force declarer to use up his trumps.

3. Singleton Kings, unless partner has bid the suit, should almost never be led, and the singleton Queen is a close second as a "don't" lead.

TAKING A LOOK AT DUMMY

Avoid leading Aces at random. Aces were meant to capture Kings and Queens. Some players go out of their way to open with an Ace in order to have a look at the dummy. This is a rather steep price to pay for the privilege.

THE TRUMP LEAD

The advice generally given to anyone in doubt is to lead trumps. It is better policy to lead trumps when that procedure appears to be the best defense. Trump leads are indicated when the bidding implies that the dummy has a short suit. Trump leads are indicated as follows:

1. If declarer has bid two suits and the dummy has supported only one of them.

2. Where the bidding has proceeded:

NORTH	SOUTH
1 ♠	2 ♠
4 ♠	

3. Where the bidding has proceeded:

NORTH	SOUTH
1 ♠	2 ♠
2 NT	3 ♠
3 NT	4 ♠

TIMING

There is one case in which trump openings should be avoided, and that is when you suspect from the bidding that the dummy will have a good suit which you are unable to stop. A trump lead is dangerous because, with the trumps extracted, declarer will obtain discards upon dummy's good suit. In such cases, attacking leads are in order. In other words, you must try to establish your tricks in a hurry.

DOUBLETON LEADS

The lead of a doubleton merely because it is a doubleton is not a good idea. The ideal conditions for the doubleton lead are in the main the same as those mentioned in the discussion on singleton leads.

The doubleton is led, not so much with the idea of obtaining a ruff, as for the purpose of exiting when no attractive lead is available.

UNDESIRABLE DOUBLETON LEADS

A-x, K-x, Q-x, J-x. When the situation is desperate, the doubleton lead may be justifiable.

THE LEAD FROM ACE–KING DOUBLETON

Holding a doubleton A-K, and desiring a ruff, the conventional lead is first the Ace and then the King. This announces that no more of the suit is held.

CHOICE BETWEEN LEADING WORTHLESS DOUBLETON OR TRIPLETON

Against suit contracts where you have a choice between leading a worthless doubleton or a worthless tripleton, by all means select the doubleton, because in addition to all other features that the two leads have in common, the doubleton does have the outside chance of bringing home the third-round ruff.

WHETHER TO LEAD PARTNER'S SUIT OR YOUR OWN

Holding A-K-J, with or without others in a side suit, a good idea is to lead the King of that suit first and then shift to partner's suit so that if the Queen is in the closed hand your partner can lead through and capture it.

LEADING FROM A THREE-CARD SUIT

Sometimes you will be obliged to lead from a three-card suit. If my choice is between K-6-2 and Q-6-2, I always lead from the King rather than the Queen, because if I lead into an A-Q my King may still live to take a trick, but if the lead from the Queen has lost to a lower honor, I have no hope for the future. In other words, a King is strong enough to survive a bad lead, a Queen probably is not.

leads against slams

Against slam bids a very popular lead is an Ace. This practice, however, must be tempered by good judgment. It takes two tricks to defeat a slam, and where it is apparent that cashing an Ace will not attain your end, an attempt should be made to set up another trick first. In those cases where suits have been bid and rebid by the opponents, it is usually futile and bad practice to lead the Ace of that suit. On the other hand, the lead of the Ace of an unknown bid suit will probably turn out well. The following examples will serve better to illustrate when to lead an Ace against slam or not.

♠ Q 6 5
♡ A 9 7 4
◇ 5 3 2
♣ 8 6 2

The opponents have reached a contract of 6 Spades. I feel that I have a fair chance to make my

Queen. Therefore, I would cash the Ace of Hearts.
Similarly:

♠ 7
♡ A 9 6 4
◇ 8 6 4 2
♣ 7 6 4 2

If Spades were not vigorously supported by dummy,
I would reason there is a fair chance that my partner
has a trump trick and I would cash my Ace in that
case. But where no immediate trick is in sight, it is
important to try to build one up before the Ace is
released. For example:

♠ 8 5 4
♡ A 9 5
◇ 10 9 8 4
♣ 5 3 2

The only prospect of a second trick against a 6
Spade contract is if partner can take one in Clubs or
Diamonds. Therefore, I would lead the 10 of Diamonds, hoping that my partner might have something
like the King behind dummy's Ace so that I can build
up a trick for him before my Ace is released. The reason is that my lead of the Ace might establish some
Heart tricks in dummy upon which declarer can discard a losing Diamond or Club.

♠ 8 6 5
♡ A 7 4 2
◇ 9 7 3
♣ Q 3 2

If the dummy has bid Hearts, the proper opening
on this hand is a Club, with the hope that the partner
holds at least the King of that suit. It is urgent to

build up a trick before your Ace is driven out so that declarer cannot obtain discards on dummy's Heart suit.

Trump leads against slams are definitely not recommended, although occasionally they turn out well; for example, where declarer has bid two suits and you have the other one well under control. A trump lead may cut down dummy's ruffing power.

The singleton lead against a slam contract from a completely worthless hand is very attractive. Partner probably holds a trick. If it happens to be the Ace of that suit, the hand is immediately defeated. Also, if partner happens to hold a quick trump trick, he will return the suit in time to defeat the slam.

Aggressive leads as a rule are not desirable against No Trump slams. In other words, unless you have a complete sequence, do not take a chance to build up tricks. It is better to wait. For example:

♠ 9 8 6
♥ J 6 4 2
♦ Q 6 5 3
♣ J 4

Against 6 No Trump I would lead the 9 of Spades, even though the suit had been bid.

leads against doubled slams

Where partner has doubled the slam contract and you have the opening lead, the accepted modern convention is that you are not entitled to your own opinion. The double calls for a certain specific lead. The convention is based upon the theory that when the opponents have reached a slam contract they will rarely go down more than a trick, and a double should not be made merely for the purpose of scoring an additional 50 or 100 points but should be made strictly for the purpose of directing your partner's opening lead. The doubler of a slam contract says: "Partner, please do not make the normal opening lead." The leads required by partner's double are as follows:

1. If dummy has bid any suit other than trumps, the doubler demands the lead of that suit. If dummy has bid more than one suit, it demands the lead of the first suit bid by dummy.

2. If dummy has bid no side suit but the declarer has, the doubler demands the lead of the first side suit bid by declarer.

3. If declarer and his partner have bid no side suit, the doubler demands the lead of an unbid suit. (In other words, you absolutely must not lead trumps.)

4. If the doubler or his partner has bid a suit, the doubler announces, "Partner, please do not lead that suit." For example, you are North and hold:

♠ 6 5 2
♡ A 9 7
◇ 7 4 3
♣ 1 0 9 4 2

The bidding has proceeded:

WEST	NORTH	EAST	SOUTH
1 ♠	Pass	3 ♣	3 ♡
3 ♠	Pass	4 ♠	Pass
6 ♠	Pass	Pass	Double

A Club lead is demanded of you.

play by declarer

When the bidding is completed, the opening lead has been made, and the dummy spread face up on the table, the wise declarer takes stock of his resources and maps out his plan of action. To that end we herewith offer suggestions which should become habitual if any degree of proficiency is to be attained at the contract table.

1. When playing a hand at a suit contract, try to estimate your probable and possible losers. If these total more than you can afford to lose and still fulfill contract, try to devise a plan to eliminate a loser.

2. When playing a No Trump contract, count your sure and probable winners. If these are less than you require to fulfill contract, cast about to see which suits may possibly produce an extra winner. Always bear in mind that these winners must be obtained before the defenders are enabled to capture enough tricks to defeat you.

Overtricks are of little consequence. Fulfilling the contract reached is the prime consideration, and any steps necessary to attain that end must be given first preference. Another good habit to develop is never to play a card from dummy, after the opening lead, until some sound plan has been formulated. Even a faulty

plan is better than no plan, and it is better to outline
a plan while there is yet an opportunity to put it into
execution than to wait until it has been frustrated by
some hasty and ill-considered play.

leading toward high cards

An elementary principle in play is that most high-
card combinations produce better results if you lead
toward the high cards than if you lead from the hand
which contains the high cards. For example:

NORTH
8 5 3

WEST   EAST
10 9 7 6   A J 4

SOUTH
K Q 2

Here you are trying to win tricks with both the
King and Queen. That can be done only if East
holds the Ace and provided he is compelled to play
before you. The proper procedure is to lead a small
card from the North hand. If East plays the Ace,
your troubles are over. If he plays small, you win
with the Queen and enter the North hand again to
repeat the process. Note that if you had led the King
out of your hand you could have taken only one trick
with the Queen. Similarly:

NORTH
8 6 5 3

WEST   EAST
K 9 2   Q 7 4

SOUTH
A J 10

Your object is to win two tricks in the suit. If you lead from the South hand, this is impossible, but if you lead from the North hand and play the 10, West will win a trick with the King. You subsequently enter the North hand and lead the suit again. If East plays small, you win with the Jack. Here again you have obtained the maximum by compelling the opponent to play before you use your high card. Consider the following two cases:

NORTH
A 9 3
SOUTH
Q J 4

In this example you need two tricks in a hurry. It now becomes proper to lead the Queen, because if West has the King and covers, your Jack immediately becomes good. If he fails to cover, the Queen will win the trick.

NORTH
A J 5
SOUTH
K 4 2

In this example your problem is to win all three tricks. If you are to accomplish this, West must have the Queen. First play the King from the South hand and then lead a low card toward the A-J in the North hand. If West plays low, you put on the Jack, which will hold the trick if he has the Queen. Note that if you lead the Jack from the North hand toward the South hand, if East has the Queen he will cover the Jack and you will then be able to win only the Ace and King.

leads toward tenaces

A tenace is a combination of cards with the middle card of what would otherwise be 3 touching cards missing: A-Q, K-J, A-Q-10, A-J-10, K-Q-10, etc. All suits containing a tenace should, if possible, be led up to rather than from.

NORTH
K J x
SOUTH
x x x

In this example, if you lead twice toward the K-J-x, you win two tricks if West has both the Ace and Queen. You win one trick if West has either Ace or Queen. But if you lead from the North hand toward the 3 small cards in the South hand, you may not win any tricks.

NORTH
A Q x
SOUTH
x x x

In this example, you lead toward the North hand from the three small cards in the South hand. If West has the King, you win two tricks. If you lead from the North hand, you can win only one trick. Consider the following:

1.	2.	3.
NORTH	NORTH	NORTH
A Q 10	A J 10	A J 9
SOUTH	SOUTH	SOUTH
x x x	x x x	x x x

In the first example, lead twice toward the honors and finesse first the 10 and then the Queen. This will gain one trick when the King is in one hand and the Jack in the other. If West has both King and Jack, you will succeed in capturing all three tricks.

In the second example, lead twice toward the honors, playing the 10 first and then the Jack. This insures your capturing two tricks whenever West has the Queen or King, or both.

In the third example, lead twice toward the honors. Finesse the 9 first and the Jack next. Whenever West holds Queen and 10, or King and 10, or all three, you will succeed in capturing two tricks. Note that it is unsound to play the Jack on the first lead. This will succeed only where West has exactly King, Queen, and small cards.

As an exercise in leading up to various card combinations, we submit the following complete example:

NORTH
♠ J 3 2
♡ 10 4 3
◇ K Q 4 2
♣ A Q 2

WEST
♠ 9 8 6
♡ 9 8 2
◇ A 10 7
♣ K J 8 4

EAST
♠ Q 7 5 4
♡ K 7 6 5
◇ J 9
♣ 9 7 5

SOUTH
♠ A K 10
♡ A Q J
◇ 8 6 5 3
♣ 10 6 3

No Trump is the contract. West leads the 4 of Clubs. We shall provide you with this minor clue, that the first correct play from the dummy hand— that is, North—is the 2 of Clubs. You should be able to win 12 tricks with this holding if you play the cards in proper sequence, leading up to your strong-card holdings and taking all necessary finesses.

entry cards

Even a player who understands the advantage of leading toward certain high-card combinations is unable to apply his knowledge when the hand from which he wishes to lead does not contain a card with which it can take a trick. In that case he cannot place the lead—that is, gain entry to that hand and thereby advantageously lead toward the strong hand. In formulating your plan for playing the hand, you must try to note whether there are sufficient entry cards in the combined hands to enable you to make the necessary number of leads toward each high-card combination. Where one hand holds the Ace and the other the King in the same suit, there is obviously entry into both hands. There are combinations which contain hidden entries, and a careful declarer will make good use of them. For example:

NORTH
K Q 10
SOUTH
A J 9 4

If you wish to lead three times from the North hand toward the South hand, you must be careful not to play the Ace to an early trick, because that will destroy one of the entry cards in the North hand.

NORTH
♠ x x x
♡ x x x
◇ x x x
♣ A K Q 3

SOUTH
♠ A K J
♡ A Q J
◇ K Q x
♣ J 10 9 2

If a Spade is opened, note that it will be advantageous to lead twice toward South's Heart holding and twice toward South's Diamond holding. There are apparently only three cards of entry in the North hand. However, there are five Clubs outstanding, and if these divide 3-2, which is normal, they can be picked up in three leads. Therefore, South's first play toward the second trick should be the 9 of Clubs, and North should win with the Queen. The second lead of the Club suit should be the 10 of Clubs which North wins with the King. If both opponents have followed to the two Club leads, there is only one more Club outstanding. Therefore, South can overtake the Jack of Clubs with North's Ace, which will be the third entry card, and now the 3 of Clubs will provide the fourth entry card. This series of plays enables North to lead four times toward the South hand. On the other hand, if North's 3 of Clubs is expended on either Jack, 10, or 9 in the South hand, North will be able to gain the lead only three times. Consider the following examples:

NORTH
A 6 4 2
SOUTH
K Q 7 3

NORTH
A 5 3 2
SOUTH
K 8 6 4

If two entry cards are needed in the North hand, how would you play in both of these examples? On examination the answer is obvious. In the first example, whenever the Ace is played from the North hand, the 7 is played from the South hand and not the 3. On the fourth round of the suit, the 6 in the North hand will be an entry card. In the second example, the 4 in the South hand and the 5 in the North hand are carefully conserved for the fourth round of the suit to create a second entry card in the North hand.

DUMMY
Q 9 2
7 4　　　K 6 5 3
CLOSED
HAND
A J 10 8

The above diagram is interesting, because in situations where dummy has the 9 and there is only one honor missing, the proper play in almost all cases is the 9 first, on which the closed hand plays the 8. This preserves the maximum number of entries in the dummy at all times. Notice that in this case, if there are no more entries in dummy and you are leading from dummy, if you play the Queen first and the 8 from the closed hand, you will be unable to capture the King in the East hand.

when to finesse

The object of finessing is to capture an adverse card which is missing from a tenace held by the declarer. In some cases the location of that card has become obvious either through the bidding or some previous accident in the play. In the absence of any such indication the question of when a finesse should be tried and when it should be refused is generally best answered by assuming that, in any given suit, any number of adverse cards from two to five are divided between the adversaries as evenly as possible; specifically, that two will be divided 1-1; three divided 2-1; four, 2-2; and five, 3-2. Declarer should also assume that in the case of a 2-1, 3-2 division the card to be captured is held by the adversary who is known to have more cards in the suit if that information is available, which brings us to the following table:

HOLDING	TOTAL CARDS OF SUIT IN DECLARER'S TWO HANDS	PLAY
A Q	11	A
A Q	10 or less	Q
A K J	9 or more	K
A K J	8 or less	J
A Q 10	9 or 10	Q
A Q 10	8 or less	10

the double finesse

NORTH
A Q 10 9 2
SOUTH
6 5 3

What is the proper play to realize the maximum number of tricks with this holding? The correct procedure is for South to play a low card, intending to finesse the 9 in the dummy hand. If this succeeds in driving out the King, your troubles are over. If the 9 loses to the Jack, the declarer's hand is re-entered and the finesse is repeated, hoping that West now holds the King. Note that when West holds either King or Jack declarer will succeed in winning four tricks, and when West holds both honors, declarer will succeed in winning all five tricks.

elementary card combinations when the opponent has lead a suit

1.	2.	3.
DUMMY	DUMMY	DUMMY
Q 7	Q 10 3	Q 7 3
DECLARER	DECLARER	DECLARER
A 8 2	A 7 2	A 8 2

In the above diagrams you are South, declarer, at No Trump. West leads the 5 of the suit. What card do you play from dummy? In the first diagram, obviously the Queen must be played. Your only hope is that West is leading from the King and that the Queen will hold. If it does not win this trick, it can never win a later one, for it will now be alone. If you play the 7 from dummy, East will not play the King even if he has it, so that either a 9, 10, or Jack will force your Ace.

In No. 2, the 10 is the proper play, in the hope that it will force the King from East. You will therefore

win with your Ace and the Queen will be high. If the
10 is covered by the Jack, you will win with the Ace
and, hoping that West has the King, you will then
lead toward the Queen, expecting to win a trick with
it.

In No. 3, there is no hurry about playing the Queen,
because if West has the King, the Queen will still be
protected and can be developed into a winning trick
later on.

ducking

1.	2.	3.
DUMMY	NORTH	DUMMY
♠ A K 7 6 3	A 9 7 6 3	A Q 2
DECLARER	SOUTH	DECLARER
♠ 5 4	5 4 2	10 6 3

In No. 1, assume that you are playing a No Trump
contract and that the North hand has no other entry
cards. You are anxious to take four tricks in dummy's
suit. How is this to be done? Since your opponents
have six Spades, your only hope is that each of them
will have three. If you play the Ace, King, and another, the two remaining Spades will be good, but you
will have no means of getting over to dummy to use
them. The proper procedure, therefore, is to give the
opponents their trick at the beginning rather than at
the end. Play a small card from dummy, allowing the
opponents to win the first trick. If the suit then does
divide 3-3, the Ace and King left in dummy will clear
the suit and you will be able to take four tricks.

In No. 2, assume that you need three tricks in the
suit shown with no other entry cards in the North

hand. Since the opponents have five cards between them to the K-Q-J-10, you will necessarily have to lose two tricks in the suit. Permit the opponents to win the first two tricks in the suit, conserving your Ace. If the suit does divide 3-2, the Ace, if played on the third trick, will pick up the remaining card in the suit and you will be able to make three tricks in the suit.

In No. 3, West leads the 4 of the suit. What is the proper play from dummy? The correct play is the deuce. This is the one way to make all three tricks in case West has both the King and the Jack. If West is leading from the King and East has the Jack, nothing is lost, because the finesse of the Queen can be taken next time. If West is leading from the Jack and East has the King, the gain is obvious.

the hold-up

The hold-up play consists of refusing to take a trick early in the hand when it is desirable to take the trick later. It is most frequently employed in No Trump contracts, but it is occasionally used with profit at a suit declaration.

The purpose in holding up is to run one of the opponents out of that suit. In other words, you plan to take a trick at such time that the partner of the opening leader will have no more of that suit to return to him. You plan to exhaust his partner of that suit and then hope that only partner of the opening leader can obtain future leads.

Whether or not to hold up is the question which the declarer is frequently called upon to answer early in the play. Perhaps the best way to learn when to hold up is to learn the converse; that is, when not to hold up:

1. When it is apparent that the partner of the opening leader cannot be exhausted of that suit.

NORTH
5 2
SOUTH
A 8

The opening lead is the 3. In this obvious case, both opponents are known to have more cards than you in the suit led, and since you cannot successfully hold up, you may as well win the first lead.

2. When the hand can be so managed that the leader's partner can never obtain the lead.

3. When there is a greater menace in the hand in the form of a shift to some other suit by the leader's partner, for example:

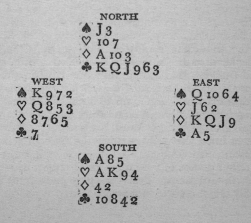

NORTH
♠ J 3
♡ 10 7
♢ A 10 3
♣ K Q J 9 6 3

WEST
♠ K 9 7 2
♡ Q 8 5 3
♢ 8 7 6 5
♣ 7

EAST
♠ Q 10 6 4
♡ J 6 2
♢ K Q J 9
♣ A 5

SOUTH
♠ A 8 5
♡ A K 9 4
♢ 4 2
♣ 10 8 4 2

South is the declarer at a contract of 3 No Trump. West leads the 2 of Spades, the Jack is played from dummy, and East plays the Queen. Unless West is false-carding, he has only four Spades and there is no danger in the hand. If East is permitted to win the trick, he may shift to Diamonds, which would defeat the contract. The first trick, therefore, should be taken.

4. When declarer can see that he is able to insure the contract by taking the trick.

5. When by not holding up you can develop an additional trick by lower cards in the suit which would lose if you do hold up. For example:

1.	2.
DUMMY	DUMMY
♠ J 2	♠ 9 3
DECLARER	DECLARER
♠ A 10 3	♠ A 10 8 2

In example No. 1, West leads the 5 of Spades. Dummy plays the 2, and East plays the Queen. It would be absurd for South to hold up, because he would then be able to take only one trick in the suit, whereas if he takes the Queen with the Ace, he is assured of an additional trick, because the Jack will drive out the King and thus establish the 10.

In example No. 2, West leads the 5 of Spades. Dummy plays the 3; East plays the Queen. It would be unsound to hold up, because by taking the first trick declarer is assured of another trick inasmuch as the 8 and 9 will drive out the Jack and King, establishing the 10 as a winner.

I.   **2.**

DUMMY   DUMMY
4 3 2   4 3 2
DECLARER   DECLARER
A J 4   A J 10

Consider the two cases above. In example No. 1, if West leads the King, assuming that there is no other suit that South is worried about, he should permit West to hold the trick, for if that suit is continued, declarer will now win with both the Jack and Ace.

In example No. 2, it would be pointless to hold up, since if you win the King with the Ace, the 10 will drive out the Queen and the Jack will be promoted to winning rank. A full-hand illustration of the most common type of hold-up is as follows:

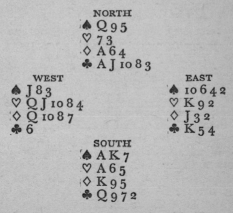

NORTH
♠ Q 9 5
♡ 7 3
♢ A 6 4
♣ A J 10 8 3

WEST   EAST
♠ J 8 3   ♠ 10 6 4 2
♡ Q J 10 8 4   ♡ K 9 2
♢ Q 10 8 7   ♢ J 3 2
♣ 6   ♣ K 5 4

SOUTH
♠ A K 7
♡ A 6 5
♢ K 9 5
♣ Q 9 7 2

You are South; the contract is 3 No Trump. West leads the Queen of Hearts. This is the suit which you fear may defeat your contract. If you take the first

trick and lose the lead, the opponents will cash four
Heart tricks and the King of Clubs. You refuse, therefore, to take the Heart trick until the third round,
hoping by this time that East will have no more
Hearts. Now if the Club finesse loses to East, he will
be unable to return his partner's suit. You are able,
therefore, to take the rest of the tricks yourself. Notice
that if you had taken the first or second Heart, East
would have had one left to return to his partner
when he won with the King of Clubs.

the hold-up with a double stopper

This is a good general rule when two key cards need
to be dislodged and you hold two stoppers in the suit
led and fear no other shift: It is good policy to refuse
the first trick. The following is an example which may
help you to recognize when to hold up with two
stoppers in the adversary's suit:

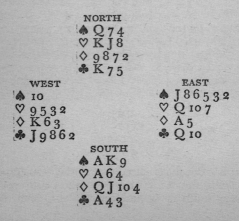

```
                 NORTH
               ♠ Q 7 4
               ♡ K J 8
               ◇ 9 8 7 2
               ♣ K 7 5
     WEST                        EAST
  ♠ 10                        ♠ J 8 6 5 3 2
  ♡ 9 5 3 2                   ♡ Q 10 7
  ◇ K 6 3                     ◇ A 5
  ♣ J 9 8 6 2                 ♣ Q 10
                 SOUTH
               ♠ A K 9
               ♡ A 6 4
               ◇ Q J 10 4
               ♣ A 4 3
```

You are South, at a contract of 3 No Trump. West leads the 6 of Clubs; East plays the Queen. You should permit the Queen to hold. The suit will be continued. You win and drive out the Ace of Diamonds, but East has no Clubs to return. If West wins the first Diamond trick, his Club suit will become harmless, because he will have no entry card to use them. Observe that if you hold up on the second lead of Clubs instead of the first you cannot make the hand.

safety plays

The safety play is very much what the name indicates. It means protection against a bad break. It is a method of play which is calculated to hold your losses in a particular suit within certain limits, in the event of unforeseen distribution.

Let us presume that to fulfill your contract you need four tricks. In that case, it would be extremely unwise for you to attempt to win the maximum if there were a safer way to guarantee that you would win four tricks. That is the theory of the safety play.

In other words, safety plays many times deliberately sacrifice one trick in order to run the least possible risk of losing two tricks. Let us examine one of the simplest illustrations:

DUMMY
A Q 10 8 2
DECLARER
9 6 5 3

In this case, if you need five tricks, you hope that West holds the King and one other, and you lead from the South hand and finesse the Queen. But let us suppose that you need only four tricks in this suit to fulfill your contract. Assume that you play in the same manner. If the Queen loses to the King, what do you do next time? If you play the Ace, it may turn out that East is now void and you lose to West's Jack. To guard against such a mischance, the absolute insurance play is the Ace first. If East has either honor alone or both honors alone, your troubles are over. If two small cards fall on the first trick, you re-enter your hand and play toward the Queen. If West follows, it must be with either the Jack or King, and again your troubles are over. If West shows out, you will lose two tricks, but then nothing could ever have been done about it. You would have had to lose two tricks in any event. A safety play which costs nothing is the following:

DUMMY
A 9 4 3
DECLARER
K Q 10 7 5

Having nine cards, you can lose a trick in the suit only if one opponent has all four, including the Jack. If, however, you find out which one has them, you can finesse against the Jack either way. Therefore, the safety play is to lead first the King from the South hand. If West shows out, the 10 can subsequently be finessed against East. If East shows out, then the 9 can be finessed in the North hand. Of course, if both follow to the first trick, there will be no problem. A slight variation of the above is the following:

DUMMY
K 9 6 5
DECLARER
A Q 8 7 4

Can you possibly lose a trick with this combination? The answer is yes, if one of the opponents has all four outstanding cards. Can you do anything about it? If West has them, nothing can be done about it; if East has them, both honors may be captured. Play the King from dummy first, and two subsequent finesses against East will enable you to pick up the entire suit.

DUMMY
K 10 7 4
DECLARER
A 9 6 5 3

Assuming that you are playing a contract in which you must win all the tricks but one in the suit shown and that is the only consideration, how would you play? To guarantee the loss of no more than one trick, since there are only four cards outstanding, it is obvious that two tricks can be lost only if all four cards are in one opponent's hand. The correct play, therefore, is to play a low card from either hand and, if the opponent follows with a low card, merely cover from the other hand. You will expect to lose that trick, then there will be only two of the suit missing and the Ace and King will pick up the balance of the suit. If the suit should have divided 2-2, you would have lost a trick but guaranteed the contract.

ruffing

As a general principle, it is not profitable for declarer to use up his own trumps for the purpose of ruffing losing cards. The theory of the ruff is to make a trick with a trump which would otherwise be useless. Where the dummy has small trumps and one or more of dummy's trumps can be used separately before trumps are drawn, they will be tricks in addition to the trump tricks in the declarer's hand. The following example will illustrate this point:

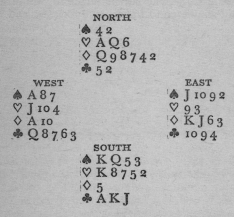

NORTH
♠ 4 2
♡ A Q 6
♢ Q 9 8 7 4 2
♣ 5 2

WEST
♠ A 8 7
♡ J 10 4
♢ A 10
♣ Q 8 7 6 3

EAST
♠ J 10 9 2
♡ 9 3
♢ K J 6 3
♣ 10 9 4

SOUTH
♠ K Q 5 3
♡ K 8 7 5 2
♢ 5
♣ A K J

South is declarer; Hearts are trumps. West opens a Club. Notice that South can lead Spades, and after West takes his Ace, South can ruff a third round of Spades with dummy's 6. The 6 of Hearts has no value as a high card but can be used to ruff out or save this loser.

South could also ruff his last Spade, but it would not save a trick, for he would use dummy's Queen of Hearts to ruff it, and the Heart Queen is needed to draw the opponents' trumps.

preventing the dangerous hand from securing the lead

There are many cases in which it would be extremely dangerous to have one adversary lead a particular suit through you. You must therefore, if at all possible, arrange the play to prevent that opponent from getting in to lead. For example:

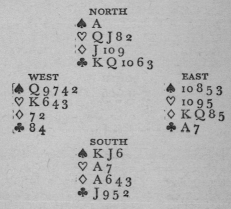

NORTH
♠ A
♡ Q J 8 2
◇ J 10 9
♣ K Q 10 6 3

WEST
♠ Q 9 7 4 2
♡ K 6 4 3
◇ 7 2
♣ 8 4

EAST
♠ 10 8 5 3
♡ 10 9 5
◇ K Q 8 5
♣ A 7

SOUTH
♠ K J 6
♡ A 7
◇ A 6 4 3
♣ J 9 5 2

South is declarer at a contract of 3 No Trump. West leads the 4 of Spades. What should be declarer's next play? On the surface it would seem that the Ace of Clubs should be driven out. But this may result in East's obtaining the lead and returning the Spade suit through the K-J. Everything will now depend on the Heart finesse.

The proper technique is to make sure that East does not obtain the lead too soon. West can be given the

lead with safety, since, if he leads Spades, it will be
up to declarer's K-J. The proper play, therefore, is
the Queen of Hearts. If the finesse should win, the
Ace of Clubs is immediately driven out and nine
tricks are assured. If the finesse loses to West, he is
unable to continue Spades profitably, and now declarer has time to drive out the Ace of Clubs and is
assured of 9 tricks.

signals

Bridge is a partnership game, and during the defense of a hand the partnership angle is extremely important. Sometimes, even with a completely useless hand, you may be of great assistance to your partner by giving him information he may need to conduct the defense. You do this by the size of the card you play to the various tricks. These are known as signals. They may be red, meaning "Stop"; they may be green, meaning "Go ahead"; and they may be yellow, meaning "Not quite sure." The following examples will serve to illustrate the manner in the methods universally adopted for signaling:

Generally speaking, the discard of a 6 or a higher card encourages partner to continue the suit led, and the discard of a lower card discourages continuance of the suit. However, if you wish to encourage partner, you should signal with the highest card you can spare. For example:

If partner leads the Ace and you urgently desire the suit continued, assuming that you hold K-8-6-2, you should signal with the 8 rather than the 6, because your signal will then be more emphatic. If you signal with the 6, it might be understood by partner, but there might be a doubt in his mind. But a signal with the 8 is more likely to impress him. Make your signals as distinct as you reasonably can.

signaling at no trump

NORTH
6

EAST
K 8 4

Partner, West, leads the Queen. What card should
East play? The answer is definitely the 8. Your partner is leading from either the Q-J-10 or Q-J-9, and
you must encourage him to continue the suit.

NORTH
6

EAST
8 7 4

West leads the Queen. What should East play?
East should play the 4, a discouraging signal. If
West's suit is solid, such as Q-J-10-9, he will not need
encouragement and will go ahead anyhow.

signals at suit play

1.

DUMMY

♠ A Q 7
♡ 10 4 3
♦ J 8 7
♣ K J 8 3

EAST

♠ K 6 3
♡ Q 8 5
♦ 10 9 6 4
♣ 9 5 2

2.

DUMMY

♠ A Q 7 4
♡ 10 4
♦ J 8 7
♣ K J 10 3

EAST

♠ K J 3
♡ Q 8 5
♦ 10 9 6 4
♣ 9 5 2

In No. 1, partner, West, leads the King of Hearts. You should signal with the 8, because you wish your partner to continue with three rounds of that suit.

In No. 2, when West leads the King of Hearts, you must not signal with the 8, because when your partner follows with the Ace you will have to play the 5 and your partner will think you desire a third round of the suit, which is exactly what you do not wish. You desire rather a shift to the Spade suit. Your proper play to the King of Hearts, therefore, is the 5, which is the lowest card you possess.

discards

Signals may be given when not following suit— that is, when discarding.

The discard of a low card from a suit in which you are not interested apprises partner of that fact. When in discarding you play first a high card and then a low card, that is drawing your partner's attention to that suit and is calling for its lead. To illustrate:

If you first discard the 3 and then the 5, you indicate that you have no desire to have that suit led; but if you discard the 5 and then the 3, that draws your partner's attention to that suit and requests its lead.

the trump echo

When a defender follows high-low in trumps, it is a signal to his partner which states: "Partner, I have three trumps and I may be able to ruff something." When holding only two trumps, the defender should ruff with his lowest trump. When holding three or more trumps, the first trick should be ruffed with a card which is not the lowest, and the second should be ruffed with the lowest. This will signal your partner that you have another trump.

discarding in partner's suit

After having led the highest of partner's suit, it is conventional to discard from the top down. For example:

If you hold the 9-6-2 in the suit your partner has bid and you led the 9 of that suit, the 6 should be played the next time and finally the 2. At this point partner will know that you have no more of the suit.

covering an honor with an honor

This ancient precept, handed down from Whist days, is generally more honored in the breach than the observance. The rule, as handed down, was: "Always cover an honor with an honor." The question of when to cover an honor and when not to cover presents a number of real difficulties. A few illustrations may help to simplify an otherwise difficult situation:

NORTH
A J 3

WEST
K 10 2

If declarer, South, leads the Queen, it is obvious that West should play the King. If West refuses to cover, declarer will pass the Queen and be able to capture three tricks in the suit. When West covers, the 10 becomes promoted to winning rank.

NORTH
Q J 9

EAST
K 8 3

South, declarer, leads the Queen from the North hand. Should East cover with the King? The answer is no. Covering with the King will produce a trick only if partner, West, holds the 10. If you cover the Queen, declarer can finesse dummy's 9 against West's 10, and your cover will have been to no avail. When the Jack is led, however, the King should be played on it since in that case, if West has the 10, it will now be promoted to winning rank. A good general rule is: Cover the last honor led from two or more touching honors.